CHAMPION OF FREEDOM

Dietrich Bonhoeffer

CHAMPION OF FREEDOM

Dietrich Bonhoeffer

BY MICHAEL J. MARTIN

MORGAN
REYNOLDS
PUBLISHING

Greensboro, North Carolina

Champion of Freedom: Dietrich Bonhoeffer
Copyright © 2012 by Morgan Reynolds Publishing

Library of Congress Cataloging-in-Publication Data

Martin, Michael, 1948-
 Champion of freedom : Dietrich Bonhoeffer / by Michael Martin. -- 1st
ed.
     p. cm.
 Includes bibliographical references.
 ISBN 978-1-59935-169-8 -- ISBN 978-1-59935-313-5 (e-book)
 1. Bonhoeffer, Dietrich, 1906-1945--Juvenile literature. I. Title.
 BX4827.B57M358 2011
 230'.044092--dc22
 [B]

                                    2010049095

Printed in the United States of America
First Edition

Book Cover and interior designed by:
Ed Morgan, navyblue design studio
Greensboro, N.C.

For Laura

Table of Contents

CHAPTER ONE

Man of Action

As dawn broke on April 9, 1945, SS guards led a small group of prisoners to the execution quarters at Flossenbürg concentration camp in southern Germany. Among the prisoners about to be hanged as enemies of the state that spring morning was a thirty-nine-year-old pastor and theologian named Dietrich Bonhoeffer. Just before his execution, Bonhoeffer knelt under the scaffold and said a short prayer. Calm and composed, he then climbed the steps to the platform where his executioner waited. A few moments later he was dead. The camp doctor, a man who had witnessed countless executions during the Third Reich, later wrote how awed he was by Bonhoeffer's bravery. "In the almost fifty years that I worked as a doctor," he recalled, "I have hardly ever seen a man die so entirely submissive to the will of God."

Dietrich Bonhoeffer was born on February 4, 1906, in Breslau, Germany (today Wrocław, Poland), ten minutes before his twin sister, Sabine. They were the sixth and seventh of Paula and Karl Bonhoeffer's eight children. Both of his parents came from eminent German families and were well established of their own accord.

Paula descended from a long line of men and women in academia and the arts, as well as in the royal court of Emperors Wilhelm I and II. Her mother had studied music under the famous composer Franz Liszt, and her maternal grandfather had directed a prestigious art school in Weimar. Paula's paternal grandfather was a renowned German theologian and professor at the University of Jena, and her father served as a military chaplain and one-time minister to Kaiser Wilhelm II.

Paula was a strong-minded, independent woman who had a sophisticated understanding of art and literature. She inherited her mother's musical ability and was a talented pianist and singer, gifts she lovingly shared with her family and which Dietrich inherited. At a time when few women worked outside the home, she took the unusual step of earning a teaching degree before she became married. For several years the Bonhoeffers' spacious home had a specially built classroom where she taught Dietrich's older brothers and sisters before sending them off to school.

Karl Bonhoeffer was one of Europe's most illustrious psychiatrists and academics, highly respected alongside his contemporaries Sigmund Freud and Carl Jung. In his career he held high-ranking posts at several leading hospitals and universities in Germany, and through his research in intuitive psychology he helped project Berlin, where the family eventually settled, to the forefront of his field. A kind but emotionally reserved man, Dr. Bonhoeffer set very high standards for his children. He had no tolerance for muddy thinking and insisted that Dietrich and his siblings learn to speak and think clearly. Sometimes at the dinner table he would ask his children to explain a concept or an idea; if they could do so without being vague, he was pleased.

Paula took sole responsibility for the children's religious education. In her view Christianity was not just an obligatory Sunday affair—it shaped everyday life. Before meals the children took turns saying prayers of thanks. In the evening their mother either read or acted out Bible stories, sometimes opening a large picture Bible to illustrate the message. Before bedtime prayers the

Psychiatrist Karl Bonhoeffer, father of Dietrich
Bonhoeffer (top), with four of his children

children were allowed to choose hymns to sing. Dietrich grew to adore many of these hymns, and some of his fondest childhood memories were of times when the family gathered together for merry evenings of song and celebration. One such annual occasion was Christmas Eve, when the entire family sat before Paula Bonhoeffer and listened to her read the Christmas story.

Dietrich's father was not a self-described Christian, and, being a scientist, he was wary of religion. Still, he accepted that reason alone could not explain everything and had great respect for Christian values. He admired his wife's vibrant faith and fully supported her in raising their children accordingly.

YOUNG DIETRICH

Although Paula Bonhoeffer continued to provide religious instruction at home, by the time Dietrich, Sabine, and their younger sister Susanne were born, she was too busy to attend to their formal education. She hired the Bonhoeffers' family friend, Kate Horn, as the children's governess. Fräulein Horn remarked that "there was never any difficulty with teaching or with their homework, both were gifted and ready to learn. All three were jolly children with whom it was a pleasure to play or to go for walks." Fräulein Horn was touched by Dietrich's affection and his generosity, remembering times when he would quietly do special favors for her, like setting the supper table before she could do so herself. Sabine also remembered Dietrich's kindness during their formative years, recalling how he would sometimes save treats for his sisters or buy them gifts with his allowance.

As with many young boys, Dietrich's selflessness had certain limits. Strong and agile, young Dietrich was a formidable athlete with a competitive drive in all games. His ambition was also evident at school, and as the youngest boy in a family of outstanding students, he sometimes felt in competition with his older siblings.

Yet his competitive spirit never drove him to act unfairly; he was scrupulously fair where others might be tempted to cheat, and he never intended to draw attention to himself—something frowned upon in the Bonhoeffer family.

Music was another area in which Dietrich showed remarkable promise at an early age. He began playing piano at the age of eight, and by the time he was ten he was playing Mozart sonatas in small family concerts. His older brothers Karl-Friedrich, Walter, and Klaus played the piano, violin, and cello, respectively. Sabine played violin, Ursula the cello, and his mother sang.

As Dietrich honed his skills on the piano he became a very good leader and accompanist. Sensitive and thoughtful, he was particularly adept at covering up any mistakes his musical partners might make. His future sister-in-law Emmi Delbrück often played music with the Bonhoeffers and was also struck by Dietrich's leadership and patience. "While we were playing," she remembered, "Dietrich at the piano kept us all in order. . . . From the beginning he heard the whole of it [and] if the cello took a long time tuning beforehand, or between movements, he . . . didn't betray the slightest impatience. He was courteous by nature."

For a while the family wondered whether Dietrich might become a professional musician. He loved music, and as a first-year university student he wrote in a short personal narrative that music was the only other field he considered studying. He relished Berlin's music scene and from an early age regularly attended performances by the Berlin Philharmonic. As he grew older he eventually composed his own music and arranged works of famous composers. His favorite hymn was "A Mighty Fortress Is Our God," Martin Luther's composition.

Reading was another of his serious hobbies. Sabine had vivid memories of him as a child sitting under the trees at their vacation home in Friedrichsbrunn, roaring with laughter as he read certain passages from his favorite book, *Pinocchio*. Often he would read aloud from *Pinocchio* to his sisters, or from another of his favorite books, *Heroes of Everyday*, which told of young people whose courageous and selfless actions saved the lives of others.

THE MOVE TO BERLIN AND A WAR

All of the Bonhoeffer children were born in Breslau, but the youngest three spent most of their childhood and adolescence in Berlin. In 1912, six years after Dietrich and Sabine's birth, their father accepted a call to the University of Berlin. The family initially moved to the Charlottenburg district of Berlin, on the edge of the vast *tiergarten* park, but soon after they would settle permanently in Grunewald, a neighborhood brimming with intellectuals, politicians, and other leading personalities. The Bonhoeffers were constantly hosting and attending social gatherings, and Dietrich flourished in this stimulating environment.

Alexander Square in Berlin before World War I

Two years after their move to Berlin, Germany entered World War I. At first, Dietrich regarded the war with enthusiasm. He played soldier with his sisters and tracked the war's progress by sticking colored pins into a map. But then, as German losses mounted, news reached the Bonhoeffer household that three cousins had been killed in combat. Another cousin, blinded at the front, came to live with the family for a while. By then, the war did not seem like such fun.

The reality of the war affected Dietrich on a more personal level when his older brothers Karl-Friedrich and Walter were drafted to serve in the army. Although they could have used their family connections to evade the draft, or at least to avoid serving in dangerous combat positions, both young men enlisted in the infantry. Walter left for the Front in April of 1918. The night before his departure, the family held a farewell concert, and Dietrich sang a song he composed for the occasion. Next morning all the children went to the station to say good-bye. Dietrich never forgot the sight of his mother running alongside the train crying out, "Only space will divide us!"

Walter's death a scant two weeks later shattered the family's sense of security. It affected Paula Bonhoeffer most severely. Consumed with grief, she was unable to get out of bed for weeks and did not resume her normal activities for more than a year. After the funeral, Dietrich inherited the Bible that Walter had been given for confirmation. This memento became one of Dietrich's most prized possessions.

The Bonhoeffers certainly were not alone in their suffering. Death, unemployment, malnutrition, and disease caused immense hardship in Germany before and especially after the war. Germany's defeat in 1918 left the country in shambles and under a dark shadow of guilt. Hoping to rebuild the country and to help bring peace to Europe, postwar leaders in Germany established the country as a democracy. Not long after the war's end, however, the depression that had begun in the United States swept through Europe, too, and many Germans became disillusioned with democracy and its supposed promise of a new and prosperous future.

Fortunately for the Bonhoeffers, Dr. Bonhoeffer kept his job and even in the worst periods the family's livelihood was never in great jeopardy. Still, they experienced setbacks, especially with Paula Bonhoeffer ill and several growing boys to feed.

A bombed house on the streets of Berlin in 1918

CHOOSING THEOLOGY

According to Hans-Christoph von Hase, Dietrich's cousin and close friend, it was right after Walter's death in 1918 that Dietrich made the momentous decision to become a theologian. At Dietrich's request, Hans-Christoph's father, a pastor in a country church, began sending him books about Christianity. Dietrich withheld the news at first, probably because he suspected that his skeptical, scientific-minded brothers might ridicule him. The decision was not unprecedented in the family—Dietrich's maternal grandfather and great-grandfather had been theologians—but the Bonhoeffers were scientists and jurists. For someone of Dietrich's background and caliber, especially coming out of Grunewald, theology as a profession was not held in high regard.

It was not until his church confirmation in 1920 that Dietrich told his family he desired to become a theologian. At first his brothers and sisters teased him about it. It seemed an unlikely and even ridiculous aspiration for a boy who was only fourteen, and they had a hard time believing he was serious. But when Dietrich began attending church with his mother and signed up to learn Hebrew as an elective course in school, it became evident he was serious. It was then that his older brothers Klaus and Karl-Friedrich did their best to talk him out of it. Klaus was studying law at university and Karl-Friedrich was a brilliant student preparing to study physics. Dietrich admired both of them, and he listened respectfully to their arguments. They tried to convince him that becoming a theologian would be a waste of his time and talent, but Dietrich remained resolute. In response to their teasing quip that the Protestant church in Germany was a feeble institution of little importance, Dietrich retorted boldly, even if jokingly, "In that case, I shall reform it!" At the time this claim seemed trivial, but his life would soon be devoted to that very cause.

CHAPTER TWO

A Theological Rebel

In school Dietrich was always popular among his classmates and had little trouble with his studies, even though his courses were demanding. He continued to read widely and avidly, everything from classical Greek literature to novels, plays, and poetry. In the evenings he regularly attended the theater and the symphony. The family hosted frequent musical evenings and parties at their home, and some of Berlin's most interesting and important people attended these gatherings.

Dietrich thrived in this intellectually stimulating atmosphere. Bright and self-assured, he seemed much older than he was. "Everyone who knew him at that time," an acquaintance recalled, "was impressed by his radiant nature; his high spirits knew no bounds." Like his father, he was a respectful and attentive listener in conversation, and, like his mother, he had a gift for making people feel comfortable. Yet there was a more solitary, contemplative side of Dietrich rarely visible to outsiders. Although he loved his family dearly, there were times, even during the liveliest of occasions, when he would retreat to quiet places to be alone. His sister Sabine suggested that he might have felt the atmosphere was "too narrow for his spirit." Whatever the reason, as much as he enjoyed being with others, he also desired quiet. Balancing these parts of his personality was something he struggled with all his life.

It is possible that Dietrich shied away from the family's high society activities in part because guilt weighed heavily on his conscience. At a time when many people in Germany were poor and suffering horribly, he was all the more aware of his family's privileged status. On a walk one day with Sabine he told her that he wished their upbringing had not been so sheltered because that made it harder for him to understand those who were less fortunate.

His parents worried whether he had chosen the right career path, but they kept their doubts to themselves. In the meantime, they could not help but notice how eager their son was to start college. Dietrich had an unshakable belief that there was a divine purpose at work in the world. Once, in the midst of a heated argument with his brother Karl-Friedrich, he protested, "You may chop off my head, but I shall still believe that there is a God." In announcing his decision to study theology Dietrich felt that he was answering a call—no matter what others thought. He did not know where the decision would take him, but he was eager for the journey to begin.

ENTERING UNIVERSITY

It was a family tradition that the Bonhoeffer children attend the University of Tübingen for their first year of college, just as their father had. Bonhoeffer's sister, Christine, was already at Tübingen studying biology when he arrived there in April of 1923. Still only seventeen, he was away from home for the first time. He was also no longer under the influence of his father and brothers and Grunewald society, striking out on a course entirely his own. German universities of the day placed the responsibility for learning squarely on the students—they were free to choose whatever courses interested them. Bonhoeffer attended Tübingen

The library building at the University of Tübingen

for two semesters and found much that interested him. He took a wide variety of courses related to religion and philosophy, and his fluency in Hebrew allowed him to take classes normally reserved for older students. He enjoyed most of his courses, as well as debates with fellow students on the social issues of the day.

Like his father, Bonhoeffer joined Tübingen's *Igel* fraternity. (*Igel*, pronounced "eagle," means "hedgehog.") He did not take his affiliation with the fraternity very seriously, though he did make a number of friends, and his presence was far from unnoticed. Now grown to over six feet tall, with wide shoulders and powerful arms and legs, he made an immediate physical impression, one amplified by his formidable intellect. His self-confidence made him seem far older than seventeen, an image one of his fraternity brothers later alluded to:

> In nearly every field that meant anything to me he was already at home on his own account and stood for something, whether as theologian, musician, philosopher . . . or as a companionable, physically agile and tough young man. . . . He already had a sharp nose for essentials and a determination to get to the bottom of things. He was . . . very natural and receptive to new ideas. . . . He was capable of subtly teasing people and had a great deal of humor.

VISITING ROME, TURNING TO FAITH

In the winter of 1924, while Bonhoeffer was still in his first year at Tübingen, an accident occurred that forced him to suspend his studies. While ice-skating, he fell and suffered a severe concussion. He celebrated his eighteenth birthday in the hospital, and his worried parents rushed to town when they heard about his injury. He took advantage of the timing to ask them something he had been pondering for a while: if he could spend a term studying in Rome when he recovered. They granted his wish, and that spring Bonhoeffer and his brother Klaus left on a three-month visit to Italy. Delighted by the prospect of visiting Rome, Dietrich taught himself as much Italian as he could in the weeks before they left.

St. Peter's Basilica from the River Tiber. The iconic dome dominates the skyline of Rome.

On their way to Rome the two brothers met a young Catholic priest in Bologna who offered to serve as a religious tour guide. Klaus was not interested—the architecture and history of the great city were what intrigued him. Dietrich, always curious and open-minded, eagerly accepted the young priest's offer. He was moved by what he discovered. The churches of Rome, especially St. Peter's, were a revelation. The magnificent architecture, the colorful pageantry, the music, and most of all, the devotion and diversity of the worshippers—caused him to rethink what the church should be.

Despite his decision to become a theologian, Bonhoeffer had spent little time in church and had not directed very much thought or energy toward it. It was a strong religious faith through training at home—not his experience at church—that led him to theology. His visit to Rome coincided with the Easter season, a time when worshippers and priests from all over the world descended on the city. Seeing the vast throngs of Christians made an unforgettable impression on him. Here were thousands of people whose faith in God connected them. In his diary he wrote, "white, black, yellow faces, the sense of the Church's universality is immensely powerful." He wrote that it was here that he began to understand the concept of the church for the first time.

Bonhoeffer's classes in Rome were not particularly challenging, so the two brothers explored the city thoroughly in their spare time. They also made excursions to Sicily and even visited North Africa for ten days. It was an adventurous three months, and it marked the beginning of Bonhoeffer's preoccupation with the idea of the Church as a community, a preoccupation that would greatly influence the development of his theology at university and later as a pastor.

STUDYING IN BERLIN

After his summer of travel Bonhoeffer transferred to the University of Berlin. He spent the next three years living at home and taking classes. At that point he, Sabine, and their little sister Susi were the only Bonhoeffer children still living at home. Soon there would just be two of them left—later that year Sabine became engaged to a brilliant young lawyer named Gerhard Leibholz. The whole family liked Gerhard, but Sabine's parents had a serious concern. Although Gerhard was a Christian, his father was Jewish. The Bonhoeffers had nothing against Jews— many of their friends were Jewish—but Jews were increasingly being regarded with contempt in Germany, and Sabine's parents were uneasy about the couple's future. World War I had left the country mired in economic depression and political chaos, and Jews became a popular scapegoat for Germany's woes. Despite their concern, Sabine's parents gave their blessing to the engagement and the couple was married. When their first child, Marianne, was born, Dietrich was delighted to become her godfather.

Meanwhile, Bonhoeffer plunged into his studies in Berlin. He read all the writings of Martin Luther, even memorizing passages that struck him as most important. An exceptionally promising student, he did not always see eye-to-eye with his professors. Berlin had been the leading center for theological study in the world for years, and the university boasted a faculty of world-renowned theologians. Most of them were proponents of liberal theology, which holds that the beliefs about God expressed in the Bible do not represent absolute truth; instead, those ideas are rooted in the historical-cultural context of the time they were written. Many of his professors even went so far as to renounce God's existence from their lecterns.

To their annoyance Bonhoeffer had become intrigued by the writings of a Swiss theologian named Karl Barth, who was a devout Christian.

Barth was a professor at the University of Göttingen. Bonhoeffer's cousin, Hans-Christoph von Hase, had taken a course under Barth at Göttingen and was so impressed that he switched his course of study from physics to theology. Hans-Christoph sent some of his lecture notes to Bonhoeffer, who subsequently became captivated by Barth's ideas.

For Bonhoeffer, Barth's appeal was his directness. Unlike most of the professors in Berlin, Barth did not focus on relatively abstract ideas. Instead, he was concerned with the spiritual aspects of God; how individual Christians could approach God and under-

Swiss theologian Karl Barth

stand his will. Always eager to get to the heart of matters, Bonhoeffer was far more interested in the faith's truth claims and its relevance for all times than in its cultural history and practice. Barth's search for spiritual truth in the modern world excited Bonhoeffer, and the budding theologian considered Barth's insight a window into a new and fruitful area of theological inquiry.

Theology professors at the University of Berlin clashed with Barth, making Bonhoeffer somewhat of a theological rebel because of his esteem for Barth. Barely twenty years old, he shocked his classmates by arguing at length with professors during seminars, something that was unheard of. (At the time, university lectures were highly formal, and the format allowed for very little open discussion or criticism.) After observing Bonhoeffer convincingly defend Barth in a debate with the legendary professor Adolf von Harnack, one of his classmates admitted to feeling a secret thrill at this demonstration of "free, critical and independent theological thought."

As an adolescent Bonhoeffer had sharpened his rhetorical skills in arguments with his brothers and in conversations with his father at the supper table; now, he was defending his beliefs against his professors. His brilliance and his natural charisma caught the attention of his peers. They were eager to listen to his ideas on faith and religion and were drawn to his self-confidence, his enthusiasm, and his willingness to help them in their studies. This role was somewhat peculiar because Bonhoeffer was in many ways an introvert. Making close friends was not something that came naturally to him in his youth, and many of his friendships had come about largely through family. Still, people always seemed to enjoy his company.

EARLY PARISH WORK AND GRADUATION

The Bonhoeffer family assumed Dietrich would pursue a career as an academic like his grandfather. Initially he, too, thought that his career would be in academics, but after his visit to Rome and subsequently his church involvement in Berlin, he developed an interest in parish work. His first brush with being a pastor came through a university assignment to organize a children's study group, which he did at a church in his home neighborhood, Grunewald. Typically, he threw himself into the job wholeheartedly. Every Sunday he retold Bible stories, using some of the same storytelling techniques his mother had used when he was child. He persuaded his younger sister Susi to assist him, and sometimes they took the children on outings or invited them to their house to play games. Bonhoeffer's classes became popular and attendance soared. He discovered that he liked working with young people. Theological concepts, he told a friend, were worthless unless they could be explained to small children.

Bonhoeffer did not limit his pastoral work to young children. One night a week he invited high school students to meet with him at the Bonhoeffer home. He might begin the evening by reading a short piece about a religious, political, or ethical topic. Afterward he would moderate a lively discussion, and often the group would end their evening by attending an opera, concert, or other cultural offering. The young people Bonhoeffer worked with appreciated his respect for their opinions, as well as his openness and generosity. His intention was to cultivate a sense of community, to demonstrate that Christianity was more than a code of religious beliefs or a concept of God—it was a way of life. Faith, he argued, meant living fully in the world—not separating oneself from it. "If you want to find God, be faithful to the world," he would often preach.

Bonhoeffer delivered his first sermon on October 18, 1925, at the Stahnsdorfer Church just outside Berlin. His mother was in attendance and she may have been among those shocked by what they heard. In Bonhoeffer's eyes many Christians in Germany, even the more devout church members, had become complacent in their faith. His vision posed a great challenge to them. "Christianity means decision, change, denial, yes, even hostility to the past, to the men of old. Christ smashes the men of the past into total ruin. He smites and cuts through with his sword to the innermost nerve . . . where the apparently most noble feelings meet with a satisfied morality."

He continued developing his views through his work in the church and his studies at university, where he made rapid progress toward obtaining his degree. In 1927, at the age of twenty-one, he earned a doctorate with highest honors. His dissertation, "The Communion of Saints," presented his view of the church as a community of believers working together to fulfill God's will on earth.

A narrow, winding street in Barcelona's Gothic Quarter

Having earned his doctorate, Bonhoeffer found himself at a crossroads: would he build upon his experience as a pastor and enter the ministry, or, as his parents hoped, remain in academia? At the time he was undecided about which course to plot. Later that year he received an offer to serve for one year as an assistant minister at a German church in Barcelona, Spain, and he accepted it. Reflecting on his decision to go to Barcelona, he wrote, "This offer seemed to bring to fruition a wish that had grown stronger and stronger over the past few years and months, namely, to stand on my own feet for a longer period completely outside my previous circle of acquaintances."

His experience in Barcelona would affirm and intensify this desire to venture out into the world. It also set in motion a phase of teetering between ministry and academia. After Barcelona would come two years of postgraduate study, first back in Berlin and then in New York; then came two years split between clerical work and lecturing at the University of Berlin; followed by almost two years in the service of two German congregations in London. Travel and diverse experiences would broaden Bonhoeffer's understanding of the Christian faith and deepen his commitment to achieving that picture of the church that he had first glimpsed in Rome.

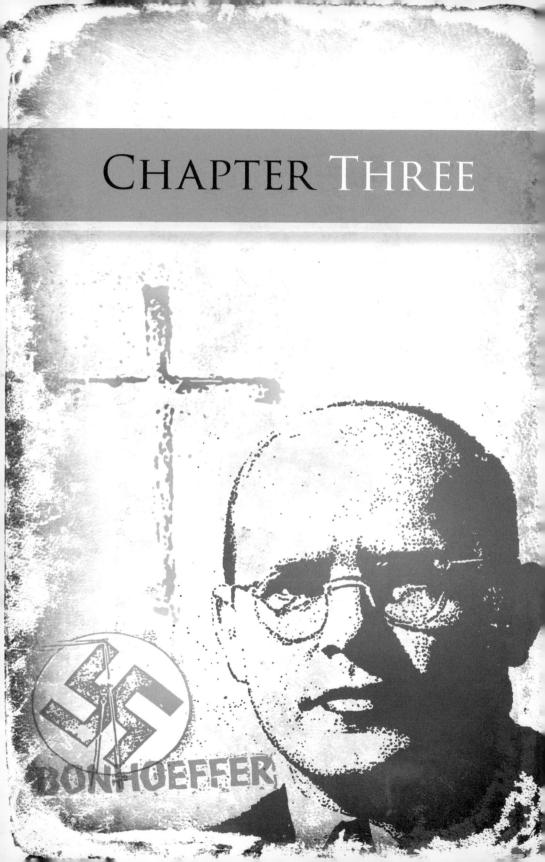

CHAPTER THREE

BARCELONA AND NEW YORK

Bonhoeffer left Berlin for Barcelona in early 1928. On the way he stopped in Paris. After a week of exploring the city and soaking up as much of its arts, culture, and history as he could, he boarded a train bound for his new home. His supervisor, Pastor Friedrich Olbricht, picked him up at the station. Bonhoeffer commenced work at the church almost immediately. His duties included directing a children's program and preaching when Olbricht was away.

Bonhoeffer entered a world in Barcelona that was markedly different from his in Berlin. The congregation consisted mainly of small businessmen and their families. Aside from a few members, most of them led simpler lives and were only vaguely interested in the arts, literature, or politics. And unlike Bonhoeffer, who immediately set about learning Spanish, they had little curiosity about the country they were living in. Instead they remained focused on their homeland, reading German newspapers, rarely speaking with their Spanish neighbors, and generally keeping a distance from the world around them. Regarding religion and the church, their faiths were lackluster, and they had little desire to see substantial change.

In Barcelona Bonhoeffer's idealism ran up against reality. Worshippers at his church were far from the "communion of saints" he had envisioned for his thesis. Still, Bonhoeffer did not disparage or blame them. He worked hard at ministering to their needs, filling his days with church-related activities. One of the first things he did was visit the homes of all his parishioners. His skill at listening served him well, and gradually he endeared himself to the parishioners. They admired his sincerity and respected his eagerness—even if they did not quite understand him.

As he had in Berlin, Bonhoeffer started a Sunday school for children. On the first day only one child showed up, shaking his self-confidence. But by the third Sunday that number had climbed to thirty children, and attendance remained at or above that mark throughout his stay in Barcelona. Also as in Berlin, he began a study group for older students. They gathered in his small apartment several times a month and discussed weighty topics like sin, evil, and God's role in the universe. Again, he made a lasting impact. Years after he had left Barcelona and returned to Berlin, some of the boys in his classes continued to write to him. Several even visited him.

Bonhoeffer certainly enjoyed working with young people, but his passion lay in writing and giving sermons. Fortunately, Pastor Olbricht gave him far more responsibility than a typical twenty-two-year-old assistant might expect. During 1928 Bonhoeffer preached nineteen times and was quite pleased to discover he had a knack for composing and delivering sermons. He considered preaching a pastor's most important responsibility and devoted enormous energy to this aspect of his ministry, usually spending the entire week prior to Sunday preparing his message. His goal was to say something important, to shake his congregation out of complacency and inspire them to think about faith in new ways. The congregation responded positively, doubling in size.

Whether or not the businessmen and their families fully understood or even cared about the difficult theological concepts Bonhoeffer preached, they were impressed by his energy and enthusiasm. The more he preached the more he realized that people regard a pastor's personality and example as importantly as they do his or her words. He introduced ideas from the pulpit and then enacted them. He talked often of how Christians needed to be involved in the world. He also stressed the importance of spending a few minutes alone in silence each day, listening for God's voice. Bonhoeffer practiced this regularly. He believed that during moments of quiet, God makes his will known to man—and that it is the Christian's duty to follow that will. In December 1928 he instructed the boys in his study group, "What this will is, the occasion will tell you; it is only necessary to understand that one's own will must always be abandoned to the divine will, that one's own will must be given up, if the divine will is to be manifested."

About to turn twenty-three in February, he was still two years shy of qualifying for ordination in Germany as a full-fledged minister. The congregation in Barcelona invited him to stay at their church and continue his work, but Bonhoeffer had already chosen to move back to Berlin and finish completing the qualifications required to be a professor. He had not made up his mind about one path or the other; despite his success at the church in Barcelona he did not want to give up on the possibility of a career in academia just yet. He arrived back home just after his birthday and began working on his post-doctoral thesis.

BACK IN BERLIN

The post-doctoral degree, or *Habilitation*, is undertaken with advising from a professor. Although his advisor tried to steer him in a different direction, Bonhoeffer chose as his topic the same subject matter as he had in "The Communion of Saints"—the role of the church in society. His thesis, "Act and Being," submitted that the church is a community that not only believes in the gospel but acts on that belief by loving and helping one another—even when others are not members of the church. *The Communion of Saints* was published as a book in 1929; *Act and Being* eventually became a book, too. Neither work was read widely at the time. Few people believed that someone so young could have anything important to say. It was only after Bonhoeffer's death that his ideas attracted attention.

By February of 1930 Bonhoeffer had completed his thesis. He defended it that summer, and the university accepted it in July, making him certified to become a permanent lecturer. He had a post as volunteer assistant lecturer, but, characteristically, he was already contemplating another move—possibly to India, where he dreamed of visiting Mahatma Gandhi, the leader of India's independence movement. Gandhi's use of nonviolence to fight oppression, as well as his spiritual communities, intrigued Bonhoeffer. He suspected that observing Gandhi firsthand would provide valuable spiritual and leadership insight.

Gandhi's use of nonviolence to fight oppression, as well as his spiritual communities, intrigued Bonhoeffer.

At the time Gandhi was not the well-known figure he would become in later years, and Bonhoeffer's fascination with him puzzled his friends and colleagues, especially his parents. But he had an ally in his paternal grandmother, a remarkably free-spirited and open-minded woman. Although she was in her late eighties, the two corresponded often. When Bonhoeffer arrived in Barcelona she had written him with a suggestion that he kept turning over in his mind. "In your place I should try some time or other to get to know the contrasting world of the East, I am thinking of India, Buddha, and his world." She even sent some money for such a trip.

Shortly after the university accepted his dissertation, an unexpected opportunity shifted Bonhoeffer's attention away from the East and Gandhi. He was offered a Sloane Fellowship to study for a year at Union Theological Seminary in New York City. The decision was difficult. He doubted whether American theologians would have much to teach him, as he had already been under the tutelage of the world's foremost theologians in Berlin. In spite of that, his appetite for seeing the world and enlarging his realm of experience trumped his skepticism about the quality of education at Union, and he accepted the scholarship.

At the time, Germany's image in the West was tainted. The Versailles Treaty, signed in 1919 by the United States and most European countries, declared Germany responsible for World War I and stipulated that it pay reparations for war damages. This proved a huge setback to Germany's recovery after the war. Many Germans were upset by the agreement and discontented with America, which had led the way in setting the treaty's conditions. Compounding these tensions was the Great Depression, which spread outside the United States and put most of the world, especially Germany, in severe economic hardship.

Given the knotty relationship between Germany and America, Bonhoeffer was unsure of how he would be received in the United States. He made a concerted effort to ensure that his transition to life in New York went smoothly, and he would take several opportunities to publicly explain the current situation from Germany's perspective. Upon his arrival and throughout his stay in America, however, he was surprised to find that many Americans sympathized with Germany's unfavorable predicament and that the two countries' political troubles were not a hindrance to his relationships.

In fact, a circle of friendship quickly formed between Bonhoeffer, two Americans, and two other Europeans. One of the Americans was named Frank Fisher, who would become a very close friend of Bonhoeffer's and whose perspective would change the way he approached ministry and theology altogether.

AT UNION IN NEW YORK

Bonhoeffer arrived in New York in September of 1930. As he expected, he found theology there lackluster compared to Berlin. But another aspect of the seminary did capture his imagination. The faculty members at Union Seminary advocated what came to be known as the "Social Gospel," a belief that Christianity must become involved with people's daily lives. Students were expected to show a practical concern for the community, and many of their required courses explored the day's political and social problems with a Biblical perspective.

As someone who preached action and the need to be faithful to the world, Bonhoeffer plunged enthusiastically into the study of American culture. He visited schools, playgrounds, children's courts, youth organizations, and other kinds of welfare agencies. In general, the Christian churches he visited disappointed him. Most, he concluded, were not so much communities of believing Christians following the Gospel as they were social clubs.

This was not the case in Harlem, a neighborhood in Upper Manhattan, near Union Seminary, where predominantly African Americans lived. Ever open to new experiences, Harlem intrigued Bonhoeffer in large part because he knew so little about it. His link to the neighborhood was a fellow

Union Theological Seminary in New York City around 1910

theologian named Frank Fisher, one of the few African American students at the seminary. Racism was common in America then, but this was no deterrent to Bonhoeffer and Fisher becoming close friends. Once, when a group of students went to eat at a restaurant, Fisher was refused service because of his race. In protest, Bonhoeffer indignantly led the whole group onto the street.

Fisher invited Bonhoeffer home to meet his family in Harlem. As he explored Harlem's Baptist churches, something about the combination of deep faith and the music touched him deeply. Like the Catholics he had seen in Rome, these were people who truly believed. And the music reminded him of how he felt when he sang hymns as a child—that faith could be both emotional and intellectual. For six months Bonhoeffer attended an African American church nearly every Sunday. He taught Sunday school and Bible classes and developed an abiding love of gospel music. Later, he would look back on the experience as "one of the most pleasing and significant events of my American visit."

Fisher was one of the two American friends Bonhoeffer made between 1930 and 1931. The other was Paul Lehmann. Lehmann and his wife, Marion, opened their home to Bonhoeffer, cooked him meals, took him to movies, and even taught him to drive. Lehmann was working on his thesis, and the two enjoyed discussing and debating theology. Bonhoeffer enjoyed debating with Lehmann because, unlike most of the students at Union, Lehmann had an understanding of European theology. And like most people who got to know Bonhoeffer, Lehmann felt he was in the presence of a man destined for leadership. "His impressive physique lent support to a resolute bearing and firmness of purpose that simply took command, uncalculated command, of every situation in which he was present."

Lehmann was equally impressed by Bonhoeffer's lack of pretense and his ability to relate comfortably with people from all walks of life. Rounding out the circle of transatlantic friendship were two other Europeans. Erwin Sutz was a scholarship student from Switzerland who had studied under Karl Barth and remained in contact with him. Besides their mutual admiration of Barth, Bonhoeffer and Sutz both spoke German, played piano, and loved music. During Christmas of 1930 they took a short vacation to Cuba together.

The other European was a French scholarship student named Jean Lasserre. Like most Germans, Bonhoeffer was bitter toward the French government over the harsh terms they imposed in the Versailles Treaty after World War I. Although his relationship with Lasserre got off to a chilly beginning, they eventually became dear friends. According to Lasserre the breakthrough came when they went to see the World War I movie, *All Quiet on the Western Front*. For some reason the audience identified with the German soldiers, laughing and cheering when French soldiers were killed. Realizing how painful this must have been for Lasserre to watch, Bonhoeffer could not do enough to console him afterwards. Lassere was touched by his thoughtfulness, and their friendship blossomed from then on.

A shy, thoughtful man, Lasserre was passionately opposed to war. He was also part of the ecumenical movement, an international campaign promoting unity and cooperation between different churches and denominations. For one, Lasserre's pacifism and ecumenism prompted Bonhoeffer to reconsider the German concept of patriotism. Most Germans strongly believed that unquestioning patriotism was a Christian virtue, and the Nazis would appeal to this sentiment to gain support and later to justify war. Lasserre tried to persuade Bonhoeffer that pacifism had a strong theological foundation in the Bible, especially in the Sermon on the Mount, which he believed was a guide to how one should live as a Christian. Lasserre also argued that being a Christian meant "quite simply" that one followed the commandments of Jesus, regardless of international boundaries. Bonhoeffer never became a principled pacifist, but Lasserre's example helped inspire him to become a vocal advocate for peace.

ON THE OPEN ROAD

After the academic year ended, Bonhoeffer and Lasserre enjoyed one last great adventure. Curious to see more of the United States and Mexico, they bought a beat-up Oldsmobile and drove it all the way to Mexico City, camping out along the way when they could not find lodging. Easy-going and adaptable, Bonhoeffer proved to be the perfect traveling companion.

"He had an extraordinarily even temperament, capable of ignoring anger, anxiety and discouragement," recalled Lasserre. "He seemed unable to despise anyone." When they reached Mexico City, Bonhoeffer and Lasserre were invited to speak at a peace gathering of several hundred people. That a Frenchman and a German could be such good friends so soon after World War I was as powerful a statement as any words they could have spoken.

By the time the two young theologians concluded their travels in June of 1931 they had racked up more than 5,000 miles on the road. Bonhoeffer arrived back to New York just in time to board a ship bound for Germany. It had been one of the most eventful years of his life. He would always look back on it with fondness—not only because of the friends he had made but because he felt it marked the beginning of a deeper understanding of what it meant to follow God's will. The suffering and poverty he had seen in the United States and Mexico, as well as the sincere devotion of people like Fisher and Lasserre—who seemed to be actually living the word of the gospel—caused him to reassess how he practiced his own faith. Later, in 1936, he wrote to a friend about how pivotal his experience in America had been. He expressed remorse for how proud of himself he had once been and how he had discovered a new sense of freedom and purpose by letting go of self-satisfaction.

"I was quite pleased with myself. Then the Bible, and in particular the Sermon on the Mount, freed me from that. Since then everything has changed. . . . My calling is quite clear to me. What God will make of it I do not know."

Metropolitan Cathedral, in Zocalo Square, Mexico City. The suffering and poverty Bonhoeffer experienced here deeply affected his faith.

41

CHAPTER FOUR

PASTOR, TEACHER,
AND ECUMENIST

Bonhoeffer said goodbye to America in the summer of 1931. Upon leaving Barcelona in 1929, he had yet to resolve whether his future lay in academia or in church ministry. Two and a half years later, after spending time in Berlin and New York, he was still reluctant to abandon either profession, and fortunately he still did not have to make that choice yet. Shortly after his return home he became ordained as a minister and resumed teaching at the University of Berlin, this time as a full-fledged lecturer.

Although he had only been in New York for nine months, the Germany to which Bonhoeffer returned had changed a great deal. He related the changes he perceived in a letter to Erwin Sutz, saying that the "outlook is really exceptionally grim," and that the country was "standing at a tremendous turning point in world history." The global economic depression had already left 4 million workers unemployed. Germans were rapidly losing faith in their government's ability to manage the situation, and radically different viewpoints on how to overcome the crisis emerged.

While Bonhoeffer was in America the National-Socialist German Workers Party (NSDAP, or Nazi Party) had made spectacular and unexpected gains in elections. Suddenly it had become the second largest political party in the country, and there was a very real prospect that Adolf Hitler, the party's leader, would become chancellor of Germany. Hitler promised that a National Socialist government would bring back order and stability and restore the nation's former military greatness. To increase his following, he invoked the so-called "stab-in-the-back legend." The legend held that many of Germany's post-World War I leaders had betrayed the nation by agreeing to the Treaty of Versailles. It also purported that communists and Jews had been unpatriotic during and after the war. Amid the chaos of the day—and the stinging humiliation still felt over the harsh surrender terms after World War I— Hitler's promises and accusations won him millions of followers.

Adolf Hitler (left), standing behind Hermann Göring at a Nazi rally in Nuremberg, 1928

Although the Nazis were willing to use elections to gain power, they had little respect for the democratic system. Brute force was a favored means of persuasion. During the previous decade Hitler had built his own private militia called the *Sturm Abteilung* (SA). By the end of 1931 he had enlisted more than 200,000 members, known as storm troopers, or brownshirts. They used violence to intimidate or kill political opponents and Jews and frequently provoked bloody riots on the streets of German cities. Earlier in the year, student followers of the Nazis had assaulted Jewish students at the University of Berlin, hurling them out of windows into the school's courtyard below. It was in this tense, ugly atmosphere that Bonhoeffer returned to teach. Violence would worsen still, and the racial problems he had witnessed firsthand in America gradually paled in comparison to the situation at home.

MEETING BARTH AND FIRST ECUMENICAL CONFERENCE

Before he began lecturing at the university Bonhoeffer experienced life as a student one last time. He spent most of the month of July at a seminar at the University of Bonn. Erwin Sutz had arranged for Bonhoeffer's acceptance into the program. Bonhoeffer was particularly eager to attend because Karl Barth taught the seminar. Bonhoeffer managed to capture Barth's attention when he quoted Martin Luther during a classroom discussion. Bonhoeffer referenced Luther's statement that there are times when the curses of the godless sound better to God's ear than the hallelujahs of the pious. Delighted with the comment and sensing something special in the young theologian, Barth invited him to dinner. Twenty years separated them in age, but each man was impressed by the other's intellectual perspective. Bonhoeffer was particularly struck by Barth's ability to give wholehearted and thoughtful consideration to the arguments of others (a trait later often ascribed to Bonhoeffer). "I have been impressed even more by discussions with him than by writings and his lectures. For he is really all there. I have never seen anything like it before." Although they rarely saw each other again, the friendship begun that summer would last until Bonhoeffer's death. They corresponded regularly about theology, the church in Germany, and the ecumenical movement, often disagreeing strongly. Yet Barth had a lasting influence on Bonhoeffer's thinking. Bonhoeffer always valued his mentor's opinions, even—and especially—when he did not agree.

A month after meeting Barth, and just before the fall semester began in Berlin, Bonhoeffer traveled to Cambridge, England, for his first ecumenical conference, this one sponsored by the World Alliance of Churches. He represented the Youth Delegation of the German Evangelical Church—a new rule mandated that half of the attendees had to be youth delegates—and was overwhelmed by the movement's potential to effect meaningful change. He sensed even then that a Nazi-takeover in Germany would have tragic consequences for peace at home and throughout Europe, and he envisioned that churches far and wide might join together and play a role in preventing war.

Bonhoeffer's leadership skills were immediately apparent to his fellow delegates at the conference. He was one of three young men appointed honorary youth secretary. The position did not sound as if it carried much responsibility, but Bonhoeffer made himself indispensable. Plunging into the work with characteristic thoroughness, he coordinated the activities of World Alliance churches of northern and central Europe. In the future, when he was not working as a pastor, seminary leader, or university lecturer, most of his spare time was devoted to the ecumenical movement. Bonhoeffer always had a remarkable ability to focus entirely on the task at hand, and he juggled these different aspects of his work life with great success.

STANDING OUT AND
AGAINST AT UNIVERSITY

The urgency with which Bonhoeffer carried out his ecumenical responsibilities corresponded in his assessment to the volatile political situation in Germany. Unlike most Germans, Bonhoeffer had a sense of foreboding about Adolf Hitler from the beginning. He was repulsed by the Nazis's reliance on violence and intimidation, as well as their hyper-patriotism. He feared that if Hitler took power, the country was already on the road to war. The Nazis were already talking about rebuilding the country's armed forces. Hitler's message of strength and patriotism resonated strongly with the young, and at some universities as many as 90 percent of the students considered themselves National Socialists. These figures were not that high in Berlin, but the majority of the school's roughly one thousand theological students were sympathetic to Hitler's agenda. In particular, they trusted his repeated promises not to meddle in the church's affairs once he assumed power—promises Bonhoeffer did not trust.

Public opinion was moving toward militarism and increased nationalism. Bonhoeffer's beliefs placed him at odds with the mood at the university. His colleagues considered him an outsider and regarded him with suspicion. They rarely spoke with him—the self-assurance that he possessed at twenty-five did not always sit well with his elders. A Barth devotee and a theologian of the new generation, he was surrounded by men he thought were far too interested in the past. Writing to Erwin Sutz he noted, "I see hardly any of the professors, not that this grieves me inconsolably. . . . Luckily I still have my practical work."

Speaking out against popular sentiment at the University of Berlin had financial consequences. The university paid lecturers on the basis of how many students attended their courses.

A meeting of the Nationalist-Socialist German Workers
Party in December 1930. Hitler is in the center.

Students supporting National Socialism were not likely to sign up for a course taught by a professor who advocated nonviolence. Although Bonhoeffer's first few classes were thin in numbers, class sizes increased. Some students undoubtedly signed up out of curiosity. A youthful lecturer who looked more like an athlete than a scholar was an oddity. But once Bonhoeffer began speaking, other reasons led them to stay. As word of his natural charisma and exceptional teaching ability spread, his classes became sought-after.

One student who stayed and eventually became a close friend of Bonhoeffer's was Wolf-Dieter Zimmerman. Like others, he had signed up for the seminar with reservations, and after seeing that only a few other people were in the class, he admitted to only "stay[ing] out of curiosity." In his book, *I Knew Dietrich Bonhoeffer*, Zimmerman recounts how Bonhoeffer captured his interest from that first lecture:

> [Bonhoeffer] pointed out that nowadays we often ask ourselves whether we still need the Church, whether we still need God. But this question, he said, is wrong. We are the ones who are questioned. The Church exists and God exists, and we are asked whether we are willing to be of service, for God needs us. What fascinated me from the beginning was the way he saw things; he 'turned them round', away from where they were stored for everyday use, to the place God had ordained for them. . . .
>
> Every sentence went home; here was a concern for what troubled me, and indeed all of us young people.

Ferenc Lehel, another of Bonhoeffer's students, remembered that he and the other students "followed his words with such close attention that one could hear the flies humming. Sometimes, when we laid our pens down after a lecture, we were literally perspiring."

In the end Bonhoeffer gathered a solid core of courageous and dedicated young men around him, and most of them would stay by his side during the bitter church struggles to come.

EXTRACURRICULAR SERVICE

It was not only Bonhoeffer's words that captured people's attention—it was the earnestness with which he practiced his faith. During this period of his life he deepened his commitment to the church and started praying and meditating intensively. He started several different study groups that met in informal settings. Wolf-Dieter Zimmerman's small apartment became the site of one such weekly gathering. There, in an attic filled with cigarette smoke, Bonhoeffer and a dozen or so students would discuss theological topics intensely. Bonhoeffer sought to examine matters from every angle, and he welcomed and encouraged conflicting opinions. Zimmerman remembers very little of the subject matter discussed at those meetings, but he says that was not the point. "What was far more important for us was to find straight ways of thinking and to learn not to slink off into side-issues, or to be satisfied with premature cheap answers. . . . It taught all of us to 'theologize'." When the sessions ended, usually after at least three hours of discussion, the entire group would often retire to a nearby beer cellar and discuss the issues of the day—Bonhoeffer's treat.

With his university earnings he was also able to afford nine acres of land northeast of Berlin in the countryside near Biesenthal, where he built a simple wooden hut. It was a place where he could catch up on his reading while enjoying the peace and sunshine. But it was also yet another place where he could engage with his students in an informal atmosphere. From time to time he invited groups of his most dedicated students to spend the weekend there. They debated theology, went for walks, played games, and listened to the gospel records he had brought back from America. These discussions spurred talk of organizing around their cause—the hesitant beginnings of what the Nazis would consider an outlaw church a few years later.

CHAPLAIN AND YOUTH PASTOR

Bonhoeffer became an ordained minister in November of 1931. He made little of the ceremony and the distinction, perhaps because he had been acting as a pastor for years. Soon after, he was assigned to be a student chaplain at a technical college in the Charlottenburg district of Berlin. It was not a pleasant experience. The students, mostly scientists and technicians, had little interest in theology. Nazi sympathizers tore down the notices he posted for talks, and few students attended the meetings.

Along with the failed appointment to Charlottenburg came a second assignment, one that, at the outset, seemed equally as bleak. His superintendent asked him to teach a confirmation class at the Zionskirche, a church in the rough, working-class neighborhood of Wedding. Initially it appeared he would have as much difficulty reaching the confirmands in Wedding as he did the students at the technical college. On his first day at the church, as Bonhoeffer and an elderly pastor ascended a winding staircase, the young students dropped rubbish on their heads from above. When the two men reached the correct floor, the boys refused to return to their classroom—even after the old pastor yelled at them and tried to push them back inside. Upon hearing their new instructor's name they began taunting him with shouts of "Bon! Bon! Bon!" Throwing up his hands in despair, the old pastor surrendered and left the scene.

The shouting continued as Bonhoeffer calmly leaned against a wall with his hands in his pockets, not saying a word. After a few minutes the boys became puzzled by their new teacher's composure. Finally, they grew tired of shouting. When the hallway finally grew quiet, Bonhoeffer said a few words to the boys nearest him. He spoke so softly that the entire class leaned in to

Young pastor Dietrich Bonhoeffer with
workers' sons on an outing near Berlin.

hear what he might say. He told them that they had put on quite
a performance. Next he told them a short story about Harlem
and promised that if they would listen he would tell them more
stories next time. Then he let them go for the day. After that, he
had their undivided attention.

Bonhoeffer took great pleasure in gaining the respect of such
a hard-nosed and skeptical group of boys. Determined to show
them that they, too, were loved by God, he decided to teach
them in a different way. Instead of memorizing catechisms, as
was customary, they would learn by being together. "I have based
the entire class," he wrote to Erwin Sutz of his experiment, "on
the idea of a worshipping community." In order to be closer to
his students he rented a room in Wedding where class members were welcome at anytime. Bonhoeffer shared meals with
the boys, taught them chess, and gave them English lessons.

When one boy became seriously ill Bonhoeffer visited him in the hospital. At Christmas he bought everyone gifts. He instructed his landlady to let the boys into his room if he was not around, a demonstration of trust that astounded them.

Bonhoeffer also took the group on trips to the Harz Mountains and to Biesenthal, the first time many of them had ever been out of the city. Delighted with how the boys responded to his project, Bonhoeffer wrote to a friend that he could hardly tear himself away from it. The class ended on March 13, 1932, the day his class was confirmed. The boys' families were too poor to buy proper clothes so Bonhoeffer bought the material to make the suits himself. He poured tremendous thought into his message, emphasizing that the boys would always have a home in the Christian church.

His promise that day would prove much bolder than it seemed at the time. The National Socialist regime gradually took control of the churches, and a handful of party leaders wanted to outlaw them altogether. These changes were set in motion on the same day as the Wedding confirmation, when national elections were held. Although the Nazis did not win the elections outright, they made very substantial gains in parliament. Most Germans considered the outcome favorable, as Hitler's party pledged to pull the country out of its depression—even promising to do so in cooperation with the church. Bonhoeffer was not among those who welcomed the outcome and warned that if the Nazis ever did take power, they would crush the church in the process.

Bonhoeffer in 1932

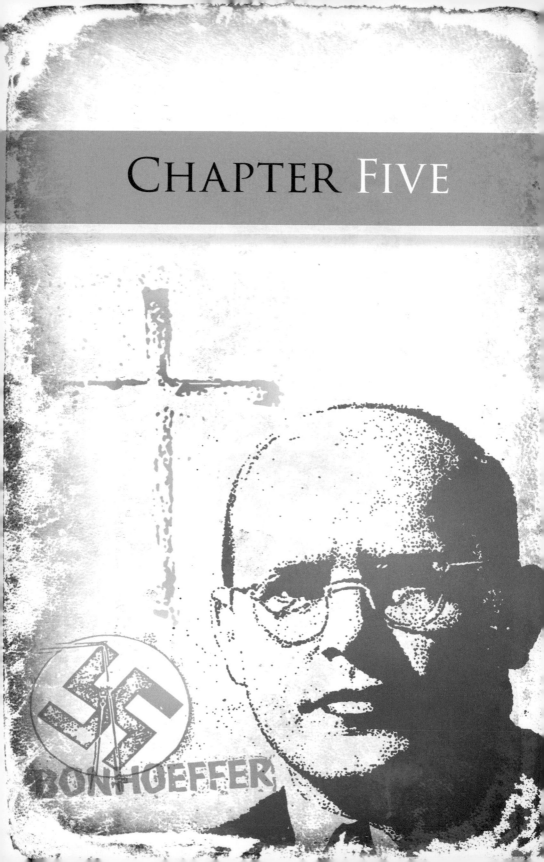

CHAPTER FIVE

Battling for the Soul of the Church

On the first Sunday in November 1932 Bonhoeffer delivered a staggering sermon before a packed congregation at the Kaiser Friedrich Memorial Church in Berlin. It was Reformation Sunday, the day Protestants around the world commemorate Luther's monumental movement. In Germany this day carries special meaning, serving to remind Germans of the cultural legacy of Luther's life. Many of the city's high-powered leaders were in attendance, and everyone expected to be uplifted by what was said. That didn't stop Bonhoeffer from ruffling feathers. From the pulpit he issued the first of many warnings about the perilous situation of the church, "Our Protestant Church has reached the eleventh hour of her life; we have not much longer before it will be decided whether she is done for or whether a new day will dawn."

Two months later, on January 30, 1933, a new day of another kind dawned when German president Paul von Hindenburg appointed Nazi leader Adolf Hitler chancellor of Germany.

Hindenburg remained president, but appointing Hitler chancellor gave clout to the Nazis, who exploited their new power to the fullest. Hitler eventually managed to persuade President Hindenburg to dissolve the Reichstag (German parliament). He then passed a series of executive acts and ultimately declared himself the *Führer* ("leader") and Reich chancellor of Germany. Through Hitler's leadership, the Nazis had seized absolute control of the government.

Only two days after Hitler became chancellor, before the dramatic events that led to the Nazi takeover, Bonhoeffer experienced a foretaste of how ruthless the Nazi regime would turn out to be. He was giving a radio broadcast in Berlin. The program was directed toward young listeners, whom he believed were misguided in their understanding of leadership, specifically regarding the concept of Führer. His message was not directly about Hitler, but the association could be surmised—the Nazis had campaigned using the Führer principle.

In the middle of his address Bonhoeffer uttered something resembling a warning: "leaders or offices which set themselves up as gods mock God." At that point his microphone suddenly went dead, and the radio address ended. It cannot be for certain that the Nazis had cut him off, but there was reason to believe they had. They would go on to take extreme measures to censor information and preempt any public criticism of Hitler. Before long, any public disagreement with Hitler or the Nazis would be regarded as treason, punishable by imprisonment or death. Troubled by the apparent censorship, but determined to communicate the remainder of his talk, Bonhoeffer published his radio speech in a newspaper and distributed copies to students and friends.

REICHSTAG BURNS, PERSECUTION BEGINS

Over the next few months the Nazis abolished personal freedoms at a dizzying pace. Only four weeks after Hitler took office the

Reichstag building burned to the ground. The Nazis accused Marinius van der Lubbe, a young Dutch communist, of starting the fire. Van der Lubbe was found guilty and eventually beheaded for the crime. Many historians, however, suspect that the Nazis were involved in setting the fire. Regardless of who was responsible, the blaze provided Hitler with a convenient excuse to tighten his grip on power. The next morning he issued an emergency decree for "the protection of people and state." It abolished many freedoms the German people had enjoyed under their brief experience of democracy, most significantly the right of habeas corpus. Now the government could arrest and imprison anyone it wanted to without a reason for doing so.

Firemen work on the burning Reichstag Building in February 1933 after fire broke out simultaneously at twenty places. This enabled Hitler to seize power under the pretext of "protecting" the country from the menace to its security.

On March 23 the Nazis effectively ended German democracy by passing the Enabling Act. It gave Hitler the power to abandon the constitution and pass laws on his own. In order to protect the country from what the Nazis asserted were its two main enemies—communists and Jews—the government claimed the right to search people's homes, tap their phones, and seize their property. In 1933 more than 26,000 Germans were arrested. Many more would later be sent to brutal prisons called concentration camps where they died from the harsh conditions or were systematically murdered. By the end of the year more than fifty such camps had secretly been set up around the country.

Two government actions in April had a direct impact on the Bonhoeffer family. On April 1 Hitler ordered a nationwide boycott of Jewish shops. SA troops harassed and assaulted Jews on the streets while other guards stood outside Jewish businesses to intimidate shoppers and prevent them from entering. Not all Germans supported the boycott, but in order to avoid trouble most stayed away from Jewish stores that day. Bonhoeffer's ninety-one-year-old grandmother refused to be intimidated. In defiance of the boycott she marched through the brownshirts and made her purchases at a Jewish business where she was a regular customer.

A few days later, Hitler introduced the Aryan Clause. It barred anyone of Jewish ancestry from civil service jobs. Since the government helped pay pastor's salaries, Franz Hildebrandt, a fellow pastor and one of Bonhoeffer's best friends, could no longer serve as a minister in state churches. Bonhoeffer and Hildebrandt had met in graduate school. Although they argued constantly, they had enormous respect for each other and often had talked about serving together in a parish someday. Franz's father was a Christian, but his mother was Jewish. According to the Nazis, this made him unfit to preach to Germans. Bonhoeffer had always believed that the Christian church was open to anyone who believed in the message of the Gospel. He was appalled at what he considered a perversion of Christ's message of compassion and tolerance. He would never accept the idea that one's racial background made a person unworthy to become a Christian. And he certainly would not stand for the government infiltrating the church.

Bonhoeffer was even more deeply disturbed by what was happening to his twin sister, Sabine, and her husband, Gerhard Leibholz. Leibholz was a law professor and had recently earned a lecturing position at the University of Göttingen. He had been born into a family of Jewish descent, but was baptized and raised as a Christian. On the day of his first class, he arrived outside of the lecture hall to find SA guards standing menacingly at the door and turning students away. Jews, they announced, were no longer allowed to teach at German universities. Sabine and Gerhard had already received threats. Now Gerhard was being denied his profession and his livelihood. Fearing for his family's safety, he bought a car and began thinking about escaping to another country.

The Nazis's treatment of Jews troubled the Bonhoeffers, but the majority of Germans embraced the anti-Semitism, or at least shrugged with indifference. No German government since the 1860s had enjoyed such wide public support. Tired of weak leaders, political violence, and economic hardship, people looked to Hitler to bring about change. A popular saying of the day went, "Better an ending by terror than terror without end." The Nazis cunningly played to people's patriotism by suggesting that Germans were a special people and that they should rally and unite behind the Führer.

CHURCH AND STATE UNITE?

Bonhoeffer did not share his countrymen's enthusiasm for the Nazis, and he was most disheartened by the tacit support that the church lent to Hitler's aggressive and already violent cause. When the Reichstag was rededicated on March 21, the Nazis staged an elaborate ceremony at a church in Potsdam. In a sermon broadcast nationwide that day, Otto Dibelius, general superintendent of the region and later bishop of Berlin, offered a theological justification for the Nazi mandate.

> When the life or death of the nation is at stake, state power must be used thoroughly and powerfully, whether abroad or at home. We have learned from Dr. Martin Luther that the church may not get in the way of legitimate state force if it is doing that to which it is called. Not even if it acts harshly and ruthlessly.

Dibelius was addressing the issue of the division between church and state, and invoking Martin Luther gave credence to the Nazi cause. One of Luther's core beliefs was that man has a dual responsibility: to the church *and* to the state. And a government that takes action, even violent action, without overstepping the limits of its power and with the intention of bringing about good, is fulfilling its function. The church, writes German theologian Renate Wind in an echo of Luther, "has no right to [seize] power over the state."

Three weeks after the service in Potsdam, Bonhoeffer presented a talk entitled "The Church and the Jewish Question" to a small group of ministers who met regularly for Bible study and discussion. He knew that some of his colleagues were skeptical of the intent behind Nazi acts, but they also supported Luther's church-state principles. Bonhoeffer didn't disagree with Luther but also argued that it was the church's duty to oppose a government that abused basic human rights. In the case of Germany at that time, he suggested three courses of action to consider. Firstly, German churches could insist the state justify its behavior as legitimate and lawful. Secondly, churches could help the victims of Nazi repression. Drawing on Jesus's Sermon on the Mount, Bonhoeffer believed the church had an unconditional responsibility to do so—even if the victims were not Christian. Finally, and most shockingly, he said, "the third possibility is not just to bandage the victims under the wheel, but to jam a spoke in the wheel itself."

Bonhoeffer's words so upset some of his fellow ministers that they got up and left the room. His speech, later published in a

The Sermon on the Mount, an 1890 oil painting by
Danish-born artist Carl Heinrich Bloch

theological journal, was the first public opposition to the government's treatment of the Jews. For the ministers listening to Bonhoeffer that day, his recommendations were too radical to even consider. It was unthinkable to suppose that the church could challenge the state. After all, Hitler had promised to leave the churches alone. As long as his policies did not interfere with church business, most ministers were reluctant to criticize the Führer. Standing alone among his church colleagues, Bonhoeffer boldly declared that Christianity and National Socialism could not coexist. It seemed clear to him that the core beliefs of Nazism were rooted in injustice and discrimination. Any church that confessed the Gospel was duty-bound to aid victims of injustice and discrimination. So by not speaking out, the churches were, in Bonhoeffer's opinion, destroying their own moral authority.

Despite Hitler's pledge to let churches conduct their business free from government interference, the next few months featured a prolonged battle for control of Germany's Protestant churches. In one corner was a group calling themselves the German Christians. Just as Hitler believed he had been called by God to lead the nation, German Christians believed that German Christianity was destined to play a leading role in Christian history. With this special destiny came the need to purge all who were not truly German. A statement from the guidelines of the German Christian movement admonished churchgoers to "Keep your race pure!" Such beliefs fit neatly into the Nazi ideology of an Aryan master race with a God-given duty to rule over others. For Bonhoeffer, such attitudes were beyond shameful, and the German Christians became his archrivals in the ensuing church struggle.

THE CHURCH STRUGGLE HEATS UP

By the spring of 1933, the Protestant churches of Germany were divided into three factions. The German Christians were led by Ludwig Müller, a man with close ties to Hitler and whom the Nazis had in mind to eventually preside over the body of Reich churches. Opposing the German Christians were a group called the Young Reformers. Bonhoeffer was part of that group, although it was never forceful enough for his taste. The third and largest group consisted of those who did not want to take sides and hoped that the church would just be left alone.

The dispute between the German Christians and the Young Reformers centered on the position of Reich Bishop, head of the nation's Protestant churches. The Nazis saw the Reich Bishop as the spiritual equivalent to Adolf Hitler. But the Young Reformers' candidate, Friedrich von Bodelschwingh, had been elected Reich Bishop in April. Bodelschwingh was a moderate, well-regarded man with wide support throughout Germany. But the Nazis, never shy about overturning election results that did not turn out in their favor, immediately began a campaign for new elections. German Christians under Müller attacked Bodelschwingh's character, and pro-Nazi groups like the German Christian Students' Fighting League organized demonstrations against him.

Bonhoeffer, Franz Hildebrandt, and other Young Reformers worked feverishly for months to prevent a German Christian victory. They gave speeches and sermons, organized protests, and distributed election posters and fliers. Their cause received a fatal blow on June 24, when Bodelschwingh resigned his position in protest of government interference in church business. Four days later Müller, backed by SA troops, occupied the church offices in Berlin. Hitler's takeover of the church was nearly complete. The following Sunday pastors were asked to read a message explaining the situation. It urged churchgoers to "feel deeply thankful that the state should have assumed, in addition to all its tremendous tasks, the great load and burden of reorganizing the church."

Despite Bodelschwingh's resignation, dozens of other key church positions were still at stake. Bonhoeffer and the Young Reformers continued working hard to influence the July elections. At one point the Gestapo, Hitler's secret police, raided the Young Reformers' headquarters and confiscated their posters and brochures. Bonhoeffer was warned that if he continued spreading rumors insulting to the German Christians he would be arrested. On the eve of the election Hitler gave the German Christians a huge boost with a radio address equating a vote for them with a vote for Germany's rebirth. When the results were counted the German Christians had won most of the important positions in the church.

Although the outcome of the elections crushed Bonhoeffer, he bounced back quickly, partly through the pleadings of his friend, pastor Martin Niemöller. After initially supporting Hitler, Niemöller changed his mind about the Nazis. He suggested that the Young Reformers try to change the direction of the church by writing a new confession, or statement of faith. After Karl Barth and others recommended him for the job, Bonhoeffer accepted the assignment. The work would be done in Bethel, a Christian

German Christians celebrate Luther-Day in Berlin in 1933 as
Bishop Joachim Hossenfelder gives a speech.

community devoted to the care of the sick in northwestern Germany. Bonhoeffer found the compassionate atmosphere of Bethel invigorating, but the job of writing a new confession was an intense and difficult task that took him three weeks.

Bonhoeffer poured his heart and soul into the Bethel Confession, urging the church to remain true to the Bible. The document also expressed concern for Jews, both those who had converted to Christianity and those who had not. It argued that Christians had an obligation to face persecution themselves rather than to abandon the Jews or any other suffering peoples. The reaction to the Bethel Confession was one of the biggest disappointments of Bonhoeffer's life. After passing through the hands of twenty theologians, it was so watered down that, in the end, Bonhoeffer could not even bring himself to sign it. It appeared to him that the Christian Church in Germany was so afraid of Hitler and so intent on its own survival that it no longer had the courage to preach the Gospel.

"INTO THE WILDERNESS"

Before starting work on the Bethel Confession Bonhoeffer made a brief trip to London, where he had been offered a job as pastor of two small German-speaking congregations. His friends urged him to go. In Germany, his chances of being arrested and imprisoned increased every time he spoke in public. In London he would be away from the influence of Reich Bishop Müller and able to continue freely in his ecumenical work.

After the failure of the Bethel Confession, Bonhoeffer felt that even his closest friends and colleagues were not seeing what he saw looming on the horizon, and this was surely discouraging. He summed up what he foresaw, "The question is really: Christianity or Germanism? And the sooner the conflict is revealed in the clear light of day the better." It would be a few years before this question came to a head. With the failure of the Bethel Confession, he decided to accept the London position. After his arrival in October of 1933, he wrote to Barth about the self-doubt and isolation he felt when so many church leaders in Germany declined to stand with him against the Nazis:

> I find myself in radical opposition to all of my friends; I became increasingly isolated with my views of things, even though I was and remain personally close to these people. . . . I thought it was about time to go into the wilderness for a spell. . . . It seems to me that at the moment it is more dangerous for me to make a gesture than to retreat into silence.

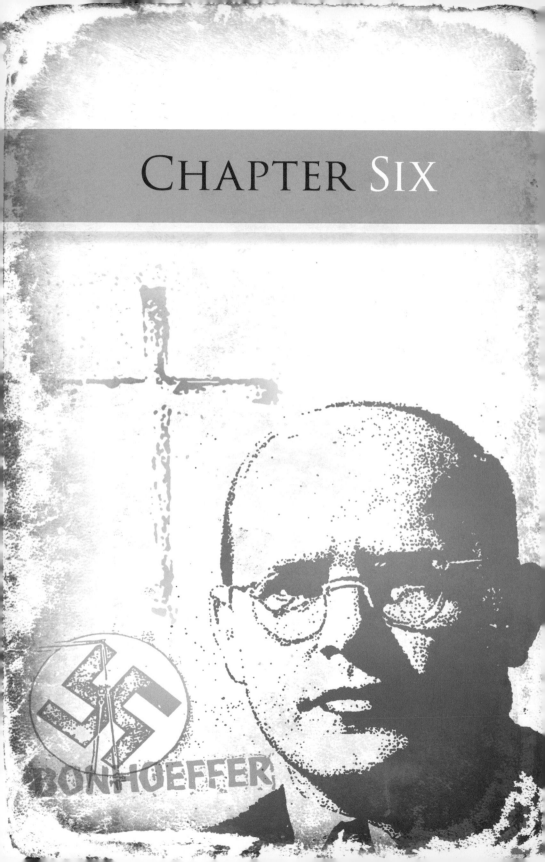

CHAPTER SIX

LONDON AND
FINKENWALDE

The eighteen months Bonhoeffer spent in England proved to be a time of renewal. He was an intellectual who thrived in the world of ideas, but he also saw the bigger picture. Although there was an unmistakable urgency to the ongoing church struggle in Germany, Christianity was about something greater than politics.

Bonhoeffer had always enjoyed the everyday responsibilities of being a pastor. As minister to two small German-speaking congregations in London he wrote and preached sermons, visited the sick and his members, and ran church programs. He also helped German refugees—many of them Jews—who were beginning to arrive in England by the thousands. His living quarters became a gathering place for church youth who came to listen to music or participate in lively discussions. And a grand piano that Bonhoeffer's parents sent from Berlin did much to brighten the atmosphere.

Bonhoeffer had hoped to share his church duties in London with Franz Hildebrandt. After his friend was unsuccessful in finding a position, Bonhoeffer invited Hildebrandt to stay with him in Sydenham for a few months. Wolf-Dieter Zimmerman eventually joined them as well, showing up on Christmas Day.

The three of them had a splendid time together. Years later, Zimmerman recalled what a typical day was like. Usually they slept in and ate breakfast together around eleven in the morning. At the breakfast table they would read the *Times* of London for the latest news from Germany and then go about their business for the day. In the evenings they would regroup and might go to the movie or the theater, then return home, where the evening usually ended with discussion, storytelling, or piano-playing until the early morning hours.

Both Bonhoeffer and Hildebrandt were excellent pianists, and their impromptu concerts were exceptionally good. When not making music together they were usually arguing. They debated theology so fiercely that one could be forgiven for wondering whether they were even friends. Their arguments would, on occasion, dissolve into helpless fits of laughter after some witty and unexpected remark. One of Bonhoeffer's parishioners, Lawrence Whitburn, recalled how there always seemed to be "an abundance of humor" in his presence. One night while Bonhoeffer was away on an errand, a scientist friend arrived at his house. Deciding to play a trick, he hid under the piano to await Bonhoeffer's return, but fell asleep. Bonhoeffer finally came home and went right to bed. Later that night, Bonhoeffer heard suspicious noises, got up to investigate, and discovered his friend snoring away beneath the piano. They laughed about the episode for months. Such incidents, Whitburn went on to write, were only "small and unimportant details from [Bonhoeffer's] life, but they do show the versatility of this most important theologian."

When Karl Barth had first learned that Bonhoeffer was in London, he implored him to return to Germany immediately. Barth submitted that the young theologian had abandoned his post at a critical time, "the house of [Germany's] church is on fire [and] you know enough and can say what you know well enough to be able to help." Though shaken by the letter, Bonhoeffer ultimately chose to stay in London for the duration of his appointment.

Bonhoeffer in the 1930s

The decision proved wise. He was able to make contact with important church and political leaders—men outside of Germany who could provide critical support for the opposition to Hitler. George Bell, bishop of Chichester, was the most powerful church official in England, and his network of contacts circled the globe. A humanitarian and international statesmen, he was also president of the World Council for Practical Christianity. Bell already knew Bonhoeffer from their work together in the ecumenical movement and had immense respect and affection for the talented young pastor and theologian. Their deepening friendship proved to be one of the most important of Bonhoeffer's life—Bonhoeffer often referred to him as Uncle George, though not in his presence—and along with Barth, he served as a mentor to Bonhoeffer. Bishop Bell had a keen interest in political developments in Germany, and since the Nazis censored news he received in London, Bonhoeffer became his source of information from the inside.

BARMEN AND THE CONFESSING CHURCH

Alongside his pastoral obligations in London, Bonhoeffer remained intimately involved with matters in Germany. He telephoned Berlin almost daily and flew there frequently to confer with his allies in the opposition. Visiting friends and family also brought word of the latest developments. Before he left for London, Bonhoeffer, Franz Hildebrandt, Martin Niemöller, and Gerhard Jacobi—head pastor of the Kaiser Friedrich Memorial Church where Bonhoeffer had preached his controversial sermon—had formed the Pastor's Emergency League. The organization was opposed to the German Christian church movement, and by the beginning of 1934 more than 7,000 pastors had joined.

Leaders of the German Christians, backed by the Nazi Party, were concerned that the Pastor's Emergency League was undermining their legitimacy. German Christian bishops forbade

Dietrich Bonhoeffer

The *Parteiadler* insignia. When the eagle is looking to its left shoulder, it symbolizes the Nazi party and is called the *Parteiadler*. In contrast, when the eagle is looking to its right shoulder, it symbolizes the country (Reich) and is called the *Reichsadler*.

pastors from discussing the church struggle with their congregations. Risking imprisonment, most of the pastors ignored the order and chose to inform their parishioners of the situation. Intolerant of their defiance, Hitler called representatives of the Pastor's Emergency League to his office. There he warned them that their duty was that of church business and to leave governance to him. Niemöller is reported to have stood his ground and retorted, "But we too as Christians have a duty and neither you [Hitler] nor any power in the world is in the position to take it away from us."

Hitler was furious. The next day Niemöller's home was searched. A few days later it was bombed. Eventually arrested by the Gestapo, Niemöller would spend eight years in prison for standing up to Hitler. He was one of many members of the Pastor's Emergency League arrested by the Nazis. The threat of imprisonment caused a steady drop in membership, and the organization's cohesion and influence gradually waned.

Still, one of the League's last meaningful acts had a profound effect on Bonhoeffer's future. The Barmen Confession (also called The Barmen Declaration) is considered one of the great historical declarations of Christian faith. Named for the town where it was composed, Karl Barth was its principal author. He lashed out against the German Christians' equation of Hitler with God and their allegation that the Nazi swastika was equivalent to the cross of Christ. The Barmen Confession unequivocally declared that Christianity's message must not be adapted to suit the day's politics.

With the help of Bishop Bell, the Barmen Confession was published on June 4 in the London *Times* and disseminated around the world. It made public that a group of German Christians had officially renounced the Reich Church. It also became a founding document of the Confessing Church, which Bonhoeffer stressed was the true German church. Signers of the Confession were not splitting from the Reich church—that would mean that it had actually been a legitimate church. Rather, they were accusing it of heresy—of breaking away from the true German church. The Barmen Confession simply reestablished what the real church stood for.

During that summer of 1934 Bonhoeffer followed the Confessing Church movement closely from London. He knew there would soon be a critical need to organize and build seminaries for training pastors. In the meantime, he continued his ecumenical work. His most unforgettable appearance was at a conference in Fanø, Denmark. There, in an atmosphere that one delegate described as "breathless with tension," he issued a stirring call to action: "The hour is late. The world is choked with weapons, and dreadful is the distrust which looks out of all men's eyes. The trumpets of war may be blown tomorrow. For what are we waiting?"

This plea may have been Bonhoeffer's most provocative yet. Earlier that summer, the German interior minister had declared it illegal to speak about the church dispute in public or in the press. Doing so was no longer simply an attack on the church, but an attack on the state. Disobeying the order would be punishable by law. It was under these circumstances that the ecumenical movement gathered in Fanø. Members of the Confessing Church movement were now under heavy scrutiny from the state, and the Nazis had sent a delegation of German Christians to the conference. Many Confessing Church pastors were reluctant even to attend the conference—much less to speak out or to fall in line behind Bonhoeffer.

ORGANIZING SEMINARIES

As tensions mounted between the Confessing Church movement and the state-influenced German Christians, leaders of the Confessing Church knew that it was time to organize seminaries across the country. Several peo-ple suggested that Bonhoeffer lead one of them, and in June Martin Niemöller extended an offer to him to take the reins of the Berlin-Brandenburg district seminary.

Martin Niemöller

Bonhoeffer was torn about what to do. He was on official leave from the University of Berlin, meaning the lec-turing post was still reserved for him. And he was still giv-ing thought to finally traveling to India—Bishop Bell knew Gandhi and had written him about Bonhoeffer. Although Gandhi was in prison, he replied to Bonhoeffer and extended an invitation to come to India to observe and participate in his religious communities.

In a letter to Erwin Sutz, Bonhoeffer expressed frustration with the education of pastors at universities, saying that their education should be at church-sponsored seminaries instead:

The next generation of pastors, these days, ought to be trained entirely in church-monastic schools, where the pure doctrine, the Sermon on the Mount, and worship are taken seriously—which for all three of these things is not the case at the university and under the present circumstances is impossible.

It seems that Bonhoeffer had made up his mind upon writing to his friend, and a short while after he mailed the letter to Sutz he decided to accept Niemöller's offer to direct the seminary. He would start in the spring of 1935.

During his final weeks in England Bonhoeffer visited seminaries and monasteries, hoping to get ideas for the seminary he was about to begin. At the same time he was keenly aware that returning to Germany put him in considerable personal danger. Just before leaving he wrote a letter to his sister Sabine and her husband, Gerhard Leibholz. "I don't want to leave—but more from very middle-class feelings of security, and these must not be taken too seriously—otherwise life is no longer worth anything and no longer brings joy. So here's to a speedy reunion!"

Bonhoeffer arrived home in Berlin on April 15, and after visiting with his family for just over a week, he and twenty-three seminary students left Berlin for the Baltic Sea coast, where they had been offered a rundown estate in the little country town of Finkenwalde. This would house the seminary.

FINKENWALDE

Up until that point Bonhoeffer still had the feeling that he had not found his true calling in life. That feeling began subsiding the more he plunged into his work at the new seminary. In addition to teaching, he began work on a book, later to be published as *The Cost of Discipleship*. In it he dealt in part with the issue of theological training in Germany and put forth new ideas on how to change the status quo. He also had given much thought to what true Christian communal life could look like. The goal of the seminary, as he saw it, was to teach a life lived according to the Sermon on the Mount. Now, at Finkenwalde, he had a chance to see whether his ideas on Christian life and theological training could work.

One of the students in his inaugural class was Eberhard Bethge, a shy, thoughtful young man who had been expelled from a seminary in Wittenberg for refusing to sign an oath of allegiance to the Reich Bishop. Bethge described his first meeting with the twenty-nine-year-old Bonhoeffer and how the young director was nearly indistinguishable from his students:

> Most of us were almost the same age as he [Bonhoeffer] was, so someone had to point him out. He came to greet me, and to my amazement invited me to go for a walk along the beach with him. As we walked up and down he asked me what I had gone through so far in the church struggle, where I had come from, and about my family and friends. This taking a personal interest from the start was quite new to me, as compared to the theological teachers I had met before.

Bethge soon discovered that Bonhoeffer was a most unusual instructor. Although he expected the students to study hard, he also stressed the benefits of recreation and relaxation. There were frequent breaks for music in the evening—Finkenwalde had two grand pianos. If the weather was nice, Bonhoeffer might cancel classes and lead a hike in the woods or a trip to the beach. Finkenwalde's unofficial table tennis champion, he loved games and played to win. Albrecht Schönherr, a student, commented that he and the other seminarians "always felt slightly embarrassed that this townsman, who was moreover five years our senior, proved to be a well-built and trained athlete who simply outran us in all the ball games in Finkenwalde." For Bonhoeffer, work and play were of equal importance. The games and the music were not just pleasant breaks; they were necessary outlets for balancing the intensity of class, meditation, and study. And unlike some monasteries or seminaries, meals were pleasant, spontaneous affairs with no imposed silences or artificial rules.

Bethge, as well as many of the other students, had some trouble adjusting to the strict daily routine at Finkenwalde. Their biggest criticism was of the half-hour of meditation required after breakfast. Many students said that their minds wandered and they saw no point in it. Bonhoeffer listened respectfully to their complaints but insisted they keep at it. The discipline they learned, he assured them, would be invaluable. His own stillness and concentration set an example of what he had in mind, and despite their frustration from time to time, Bonhoeffer's personality captivated them. Schönherr explained:

> I have been under the spell of that man who gave himself so entirely, heart and soul, whether in play or in theological discussion. . . . Never did I discover in him anything low, undisciplined, mean.

Finkenwalde is now part of Poland. Before 1945 when Szczecin (Stettin) was a part of Germany, the name of this suburb was Stettin-Finkenwalde.

He could be relaxed, but he never let himself go. It is for such a life of one piece, such an example that a young person longs. Bonhoeffer detested binding men to himself; perhaps for that very reason so many were drawn to him.

It is possible that Bonhoeffer's actions were as, if not more, influential than any courses he taught. On Bethge's second day at the seminary, the housekeeper asked for help washing the dishes. No one jumped up to help, and without saying a word, Bonhoeffer got up from the supper table and went to help her. Some of the students felt guilty and hurried to follow him into the kitchen, but he refused their offers of assistance and locked the kitchen door. Later, he rejoined the group on the beach but made no mention of what happened. Similarly, more than one student who neglected to make his bed would find that Bonhoeffer had made it for him, again without comment or reprimand. In every way that occurred to him, Bonhoeffer tried to show his students that he believed in Christ's example of service to others. He carried dinner to students when they were sick in bed, listened attentively to their concerns, and even arranged and paid for hospital care if necessary.

There was one strict rule at Finkenwalde: no one could speak about another person in that person's absence. If the rule was broken, then the offender had to inform the absent brother at the first opportunity. The practice eliminated much of the tension and gossip that can break apart a group living in close quarters. Similarly, Bonhoeffer encouraged the brothers (as they all called each other, including Bonhoeffer) to confess any resentments or grudges they had against one another. Wolf-Dieter Zimmerman recalled how "it was a great surprise to learn how we had hurt the other person, without intention, by chance, almost en passant. Now we knew what it meant to consider people." These practices, combined with vigorous theological education, forged close bonds between the young men, and their strength of community enabled them to endure the difficult future that lay ahead.

The course of study at Finkenwalde lasted from three to four months. Before the first class graduated, Bonhoeffer proposed to the Confessing Church's governing body that a House of Brethren be established at the seminary. He had in mind a close-knit group of six young pastors living together permanently in a kind of Christian commune. They would be responsible for running the seminary and also for doing mission work in the local churches. Bonhoeffer's wish was granted and the House of Brethren was established. Among the first pastors chosen was Eberhard Bethge.

As Bonhoeffer had hoped, the brethren developed extraordinary bonds of closeness and commitment—both to each other and to his vision of a caring, compassionate Christianity. The young pastors they trained, however, faced hard choices. The Nazi government did not recognize them as ministers because Finkenwalde was not designated an official institution. That meant they were ineligible to receive salaries from state churches. Any future income would have to come from the voluntary donations of congregations that supported the Confessing Church. Because such congregations were scarcely organized, some ministers preached to small groups of believers in private homes—

a particularly dangerous undertaking that could lead to arrest by the Gestapo and eventual imprisonment in a concentration camp.

Throughout 1935, the Nazis did their best to destroy the Confessing Church. In December they passed the last of the so-called Emergency Measures to supposedly protect the church. Under this measure, unauthorized seminaries were now declared illegal, and any church council that sponsored them was considered an enemy of the state. When Bonhoeffer heard the news he called the current class of ordinands together and soberly explained the situation. "We can give you no guarantee that you will find employment, that you will receive a stipend, or that you will be recognized by any state authority," he quietly told them. "It is likely that your path from now on will be very hard." Given the circumstances, Bonhoeffer told the candidates that they were free to leave Finkenwalde, but that if even one student stayed, he would continue to teach. Not a single student left—on the contrary, the next group of courses at Finkenwalde was filled.

Initially, it appeared that the Confessing Church was resilient in the face of the Nazi mandate. Yet the church struggle would soon enter a new phase: as the German populace embraced National Socialism, the Confessing Church increasingly found itself contending not only against the state, but against the rest of the nation and even against itself.

CHAPTER SEVEN

PERSECUTION

It would be a while before the Gestapo dealt with Finkenwalde. Germany was to host the 1936 Olympics, and Hitler wanted to impress the world with how prosperous and free the country had become under his leadership. Dissidents would be dealt with later. In the meantime, the government discreetly worked to divide and weaken the Confessing Church. It stipulated that the German Christians and the Confessing Church form committees and work out a compromise. Some leaders in the Confessing Church were eager to bring an end to the struggle and were open to the possibility of a compromise. Bonhoeffer, who had long since concluded that the racist, intolerant theology of the German Christians was not compatible with Christianity, believed that no good would come of committees and compromise. "Church and un-church," he said with typical directness, "cannot come to terms." Someone once asked Bonhoeffer about the possibility of joining the German Christians in order to influence that movement for good from within. "If you board the wrong train," he warned, "it is no use running along the corridor in the opposite direction."

The idea of reconciliation did not appeal to Bonhoeffer. It did, however, cause others to waver in their commitment to the Confessing Church. Standing up to the German Christians took courage, and it would be far easier to give in to the pressure and rejoin the state church. There were financial rewards, offered as incentives to tempt young Confessing Church pastors. If they would submit to an examination by a Reich Church committee—controlled by German Christians—job security was theirs. The vast majority of Finkenwalde graduates, however, refused to take the examinations. And despite its uncertain status, the seminary's doors remained open. For the time being the Gestapo did not move to close it down.

CHALLENGING AUTHORITY

On February 4, 1936, Bonhoeffer celebrated his thirtieth birthday on campus. During the celebration Bonhoeffer told the students about his foreign travels. Stories about his ecumenical work stirred them to ask him for a birthday favor: they wanted to travel. "Take us abroad!" they begged. "Let us see it . . . let us see this greater Church," he had told them so much about.

It seemed an impossible demand. Foreign travel in Germany in 1936 was tightly restricted. A group of students from an outlawed seminary obtaining permission to leave the country—the idea seemed preposterous. Nevertheless, Bonhoeffer found a way to make it happen. Using ecumenical contacts in Sweden and Denmark, he arranged for invitations from churches in those countries. Other preparations were made in secret. Less than a month later the entire seminary slipped out of the country for a ten-day visit. The trip was a revelation to the students. Welcomed wherever they went, they were amazed and grateful to learn that there were Christians in other countries who understood and supported their stance in Germany. The moral support they received was extremely valuable in bolstering their spirits.

Bonhoeffer's trip abroad angered state church authorities. The German Christian bishop for foreign affairs called him an enemy of the state and recommended he be barred from training seminary students. Since Finkenwalde was already considered illegal, the bishop's complaints had little practical effect. The ministry of culture, however, officially banned Bonhoeffer from lecturing at the University of Berlin. Since Bonhoeffer had long since given up on the universities, this move did not particularly upset him. All his energies now were devoted to the training of students he hoped would one day join him and others in the battle for the church—and the nation.

That summer Bonhoeffer held a lecture called "On the Question of the Church Community." It was published in a theological journal and attracted more attention than anything he had previously written or preached due to one very controversial sentence: "Whoever knowingly cuts himself off from the Confessing Church in Germany cuts himself off from salvation." The statement caused an outcry, both from Bonhoeffer's enemies and from within the Confessing Church. Many feared he had gone too far, that the claim was arrogant, even heretical. Surely, they argued, there was a reasonable way for German Christians and the Confessing Church to settle their differences. Undaunted by the criticism, Bonhoeffer did not retract his statement or even spend much effort defending himself. The question of which church was true to the spirit of Christ was, he believed, far more important than becoming embroiled in personal attacks.

TENSION AT THE OLYMPICS

In August 1936, Bonhoeffer traveled to Berlin for the Olympics. Always generous toward his students, he paid their way to the games as well. With all eyes on Berlin, Hitler was determined to show the world that Germany was a free, open society. He also wished to represent the nation as being Christian, and he authorized churches to organize public events, lectures, and extra services for foreign visitors. The German Christian services mostly featured university theologians and were conducted in the manner of formal lectures. These were sparsely attended. In contrast, the Confessing Church events overflowed with guests.

On August 5 Bonhoeffer lectured to a filled sanctuary at St. Paul's Church. It would be the last time he ever spoke to a large public gathering. Soon he would be forbidden to speak, write, or travel without permission from the state.

Foreign visitors flocked to the Confessing Church events for several reasons. The group had strong ties to other countries through the international ecumenical movement. But the German Christians did, too. There was also the publication of Bonhoeffer's controversial paper, news of which had spread outside of Germany and garnered attention. But there was another controversial document that had leaked just prior to the Olympics. The leadership of the Confessing Church had written a private memo to Hitler weeks before, sharply criticizing the Nazis's treatment of Jews. The letter was the only official church declaration ever to denounce the Nazis's violation of human rights.

Bonhoeffer no doubt had a hand in writing the letter, of which only three copies were made. Hitler did not respond for six weeks, and the Confessing Church wondered whether their effort had been in vain. Then, to their astonishment, a newspaper in London published an article about the memo. Two of Bonhoeffer's students and a church administrator had leaked it, hoping its disclosure would elicit a response from Hitler.

The release of the memo, as well as the embarrassment it caused the Nazis, raised cries of "Treason!" throughout the country—just as the world was watching.

Olympic Fire in Berlin 1936.
Hitler was determined to show the world that
Germany was a free, open society.

Bonhoeffer's students Werner Koch and Ernst Tillich and the lawyer Friedrich Weissler were accused of the leak. They were arrested and sent to Sachsenhausen concentration camp. Weissler, a Jew, was beaten to death within a week of his arrival; Koch and Tillich also nearly died there. The students at Finkenwalde did their best to support their brothers in prison. They prayed, wrote letters, and provided financial support to the families of their peers.

Other than arresting the three accused men, the Führer did not respond to the memo instantly, as the Olympics were days from beginning—but he would. The Confessing Church announced that the full text of the memo would be read aloud from pulpits across Germany during the Olympics. When the time came, a daring group of pastors stood before their congregations, many of them looking down on members of the Gestapo, and read the memo. The Nazis did not take immediate action, but they duly noted who had read the memo.

Prisoners of Sachsenhausen concentration camp, December 19, 1938. The purple triangle was a concentration camp badge used by the Nazis to identify Jehovah's Witnesses, as well as a small number of Seventh Day Adventists, Baptists, and pacifists. Along with Jews, Nazism opposed unorthodox Christian minorities.

Bonhoeffer saw through the veil of optimism surrounding the Olympics and knew the situation was getting worse. A hint of what was to come appeared in an anonymous sign prominently displayed in a shop near St. Paul's. It read:

> After the Olympiad
> We'll beat the Confessing Church to a pulp;
> Then we'll throw out the Jews,
> And that will be the end of the Confessing Church.

By the end of that summer the unity of the Confessing Church had begun to unravel from within. More and more, Bonhoeffer was considered an extremist, a radical theologian with an inexplicable concern for non-Aryans. Few Germans— in and outside of the Confessing Church—could understand why Bonhoeffer felt it was so important to defend the Jews. The Bishop of Württemberg's attitude was typical. Although a member of the Confessing Movement, he could not help bragging that his church was free of Jews.

PERSEVERING AT FINKENWALDE

The punishment of Koch and Tillich marked the beginning of a period of persecution that lasted until the end of the Third Reich. After 1936 many Finkenwalde students and graduates were arrested and imprisoned. Bonhoeffer and the House of Brethren spent much of their time visiting prisons, writing letters, and providing support for the families of those who had fallen victim to the Nazis.

In the midst of the intensifying turmoil of 1936 and 1937, Bonhoeffer managed to finish one of his most important books, *The Cost of Discipleship*. Although he did not set the book specifically against the backdrop of the situation in Germany, the historical context bolsters his message. The book addresses what it means to live as a Christian and has become a cornerstone of contemporary Christian literature. Bonhoeffer argues that Christians had become soft, even complacent in their faith, expecting to receive God's grace without being obedient to His teachings. He coined the term "cheap grace" to describe this posture toward God and considered it "the deadly enemy of our church." Instead, Bonhoeffer stressed, Christians must be willing to suffer innocently for the sake of others—like Christ. As a man who loved so much about life—travel, the arts, literature, conversation—Bonhoeffer did not believe in suffering for its own sake; but he was convinced that living one's life for others is the true calling of Christians.

Despite the constant threat of imprisonment, Bonhoeffer experienced daily moments of joy at Finkenwalde. There was frequent laughter, and music gave him great pleasure as always. He had taught himself to play the guitar and often led songfests in the evenings. December of 1936 marked his mother's sixtieth birthday, and he traveled to Berlin to celebrate the occasion with the whole family. For a special birthday treat, the Bonhoeffer children and fifteen grandchildren serenaded her with a grand performance of Haydn's *Toy Symphony*. As always Bonhoeffer stayed in the attic room that overlooked his sister Ursula's home next door. A loving uncle, he kept a supply of candy nearby so that he could throw it out the window if he saw his nieces and nephews playing in the gardens below.

Such simple pleasures balanced the escalating tensions between the Confessing Church and the Gestapo. Hitler's police monitored sermons, interrupted church meetings, and prohibited some pastors from speaking. Many pastors were arrested. They typically received mild sentences at first, usually only a day or two, with the threat of longer sentences if they continued speaking out in opposition to the state. Those who spent more than a few days in custody often had to be nursed back to health. Two pastors from the town of Seelow recuperated at Finkenwalde from the brutal treatment they had received after refusing to give up their churches to a German Christian pastor. Another pastor, a young Christian minister with traces of Jewish blood in his family, had been beaten badly by the SA and was also given refuge at Finkenwalde.

Bonhoeffer's parents' home where he was raised.
He often returned here for rest and rejuvenation.

NIEMÖLLER AND HILDEBRANDT ARRESTED, FINKENWALDE SHUT DOWN

On July 1, 1937, Bonhoeffer and Eberhard Bethge traveled to Berlin to confer with Martin Niemöller and Franz Hildebrandt about the latest round of arrests. They arrived at Niemöller's home just after he himself had been arrested. After being held for seven hours there with Hildebrandt and Niemöller's wife, the two were then allowed to return to Finkenwalde. Two weeks later the Gestapo arrested Hildebrandt, too. He had taken over as pastor at Niemöller's church, his preaching no less fervent and subversive than Niemöller's. The Gestapo arrested him outside of the church for breaching two new laws: he took up a collection for the Confessing Church and read aloud a list of people who needed prayers of intercession.

Hildebrandt protested his arrest, and the congregation joined in. It was one of the very few spontaneous demonstrations ever staged against the Nazi regime. After being held at Gestapo headquarters and having his home searched, Hildebrandt was shipped to prison. Because his mother was Jewish, Hildebrandt was in great danger there. The Bonhoeffers worked tirelessly behind the scenes to secure his release, drawing on their connections in the Justice Ministry. By a great stroke of good fortune, the police did not discover Hildebrandt's passport. Soon after his release, Hildebrandt escaped the country and went to London, where he became a pastor and worked with Bonhoeffer's friend and mentor Bishop George Bell.

Meanwhile, pressure mounted on the illegal seminaries and the Confessing Church. More than eight hundred clergymen were arrested that summer. The Gestapo broke into the homes and confiscated the property of dozens of former Finkenwalde students. Being a student of Dietrich Bonhoeffer had serious consequences. Bonhoeffer continued training pastors at Finkenwalde.

He expected the seminary to be shut down at any moment, but he managed to graduate one more class of ordinands on September 8. The last few days together were spent swimming, singing, and laughing together at a place on the Baltic Sea near Finkenwalde.

After the summer classes ended, Bonhoeffer and Bethge visited Bonhoeffer's sister Sabine and her family in Göttingen. While there they received a phone call from the Finkenwalde housekeeper, who told them the Gestapo had arrived. Finkenwalde was shut down.

CHAPTER EIGHT

SECRET LIVES

The closing of Finkenwalde did not signal the end of training
for Confessing Church pastors. In Bonhoeffer's mind the closing
supported his belief that there was an urgent need in Germany
for clergymen who preached the Gospel and not the message of
Hitler. Bonhoeffer and the House of Brethren had agreed long
beforehand that when the seminary was shut down, they would
train pastors in secret at remote places in the countryside. One
of their ruses was to assign students to a particular parish, a for-
mality required by the Gestapo that would not attract attention.
Properly registered with the state, the students would then meet
in groups of eight or ten at prearranged locations unknown to
the police. The two main locations were in the towns of Köslin
and Schlawe, in the Pomeranian countryside about two hundred
miles northeast of Berlin (in present-day Poland).

MOVING DEEPER UNDERGROUND

At one point a group of ordinands moved from Schlawe to a farmhouse near Gross-Schlönwitz that was so remote it did not have electricity. There, amidst the fields and forests, Bonhoeffer was as content as he had been for a long time. Compared to the chaos and bustle of the nation's capital, the peaceful surroundings were especially welcome for Bonhoeffer, even if he could only enjoy them a few days at a time. He described the atmosphere there in a letter to his mother and father:

> I arrived here yesterday. . . . Generally speaking, I really feel more and more that life in the country, especially in times like these, has much more human dignity than in towns. All the manifestations of the masses simply fall away. I think the contrast between Berlin and this secluded farmstead is particularly striking. . . . The food supply is rather difficult . . . but we still have enough. If I had my way, I think I should like to leave town for good.

An ordinand at Gross-Schlönwitz praised Bonhoeffer's ability to create an atmosphere filled with joy, meaning, and brotherhood. The ordinand, who was later killed in the war, had approached the training with dread, thinking it would be an ordeal to endure:

> Instead of the stuffy atmosphere of theological cant, I found a world that embraced a great deal of what I love and need: straightforward theological work in a friendly community . . . where the work was made a pleasure . . . and with it all, open-mindedness and love for everything that still makes this fallen creation lovable—music, literature, sport and the beauty of the earth—a grand way of life.

Bonhoeffer traveled back and forth between Köslin, Schlawe, and Gross-Schlönwitz to teach and write, but he also frequently returned to Berlin. He communicated almost daily with friends and family at home to receive the latest news about the church and political developments. He kept the Gestapo off his trail by sending messages in code and by using secret mailing addresses. On a visit home in January of 1938 the Gestapo raided a church meeting he was attending. Afterward they forbade him from traveling to Berlin. Bonhoeffer's father appealed the ruling and won permission for his son to visit his family, on the condition that he not engage in church work. Despite the restrictions, Bonhoeffer still managed to meet with opposition leaders, often inside his parents' home.

The Confessing Church faced a more insidious challenge to its legitimacy on April 20, Hitler's birthday. As a special gift to the Führer, the German Christians prepared an oath of allegiance. Pastors and those training to be pastors were expected to swear loyalty to Hitler. Bonhoeffer refused to take the oath, but many Confessing Church members did, weakening the church's unity. Those who took the oath considered it a way to voice solidarity with the nation. Bonhoeffer, on the other hand, recognized that the oath effectively gave church approval to the persecution of Jews.

SABINE'S FAMILY FLEES GERMANY

The Nazis's anti-Jewish campaign intensified during 1938. More than 300,000 Jews had already left Germany. They were required to sign all of their property over to the government—most of them left with only the clothes on their back. Bonhoeffer worried about his sister Sabine and her family. Sabine's husband, Gerhard, could not find work because of his Jewish ancestry, and escape was beginning to look like a sensible and desirable alternative. Late in the summer of 1938 the family received frightening news from Hans von Dohnanyi, Bonhoeffer's brother-in-law. Von Dohnanyi was a high-ranking lawyer at the Justice Ministry and privy to a wealth of information undisclosed to the public.

He warned the Bonhoeffers that soon all Jews would be required to have the letter "J" stamped on their passports and would be forbidden to leave the country. If Sabine and her family had any hope of escape, they needed to act immediately.

On the morning of September 8, 1938, Bonhoeffer and Eberhard Bethge pulled up at Sabine's home in Göttingen in a rented car. Sabine and her family were fleeing Germany. They packed Bonhoeffer's rental car and the Leibholz family auto as though they were going on a picnic, so as not to raise suspicion. During the drive to the Swiss border the adults switched places often so that everyone got a chance to sit with the children, eleven-year-old Marianne and seven-year-old Christiane. Although Bonhoeffer realized he might never see his nieces or his sister again, his mood remained upbeat. He and Bethge spent much of the trip singing folk songs with the children. Later, Marianne would recall that he seemed just as she had always remembered him, "strong and confident, immensely kind, cheerful and firm." As night fell and the caravan neared Switzerland, Bonhoeffer and Bethge said good-bye and turned back. After tense rounds of interrogation at the border, the family crossed safely into Switzerland. From there, they went on to England where Bonhoeffer's friend, Bishop Bell, looked after them and even helped Leibholz obtain a lecturing position at Oxford University. Not until after the war ended would the family return to Germany.

Following Sabine's departure Bonhoeffer plunged into his writing, finishing *Life Together* in only four weeks. In *The Cost of Discipleship* he had written about what it means to follow Christ. With *Life Together* he attempted to show how Christ's followers might live together in a Christian community. His experiments in communal living at the seminaries had raised intrigue among religious people throughout Germany, and Bonhoeffer was eager to communicate his philosophy behind the House of Brethren. In particular he wanted people to know that it was not a monastery and not a place for retreat from the world. It was a Protestant community where those who believed Christ's message of compassion prepared themselves to go out into the world and serve others.

NOVEMBER 9 AND THE NIGHT OF BROKEN GLASS

That mission took on a new and greater urgency after the events of November 9, when Hitler staged a massive, nationwide display of hatred and violence against Germany's Jews. That night infamously became known as *Kristallnacht*, the "night of broken glass." Storm troopers dressed in civilian clothes burned two hundred synagogues and burned or looted more than 7,000 Jewish-owned shops. Hundreds of Jews were killed that night, either burned inside their stores or synagogues or murdered by jeering crowds. Another 30,000 Jewish males were sent to concentration camps, where several thousand of them would die of maltreatment in a matter of weeks.

A ruined synagogue in Munich after *Kristallnacht*, or Night of the Broken Glass

Secluded in Gross-Schlönwitz, Bonhoeffer did not receive news of the atrocities until the next morning. At the time he was reading in the book of Psalms and one passage, Psalm 74, was eerily prophetic. Next to the line, "they burned all the meeting places of God in the land," he wrote, "November 9." Some of his ordinands wondered whether the Nazi pogrom might be part of a divine curse on the Jews. Bonhoeffer sharply rejected their question: "if the synagogues burn today," he responded, "the churches will be on fire tomorrow."

In all of Germany there was not a single display of public opposition to Kristallnacht. Bonhoeffer was appalled. One Protestant church leader, Bishop Martin Sasse, even insinuated that Martin Luther would have commended the massacre. "On November 10, 1938, on Luther's birthday, the synagogues are burning in Germany." Although most people felt uneasy about what had happened, the nation's churches remained silent. This silence only aggravated Bonhoeffer's disgruntlement with the Confessing Church. With so many of its members willing to sign loyalty oaths to a criminal regime, it seemed to him as if people were far too concerned with their church's survival—even if what survived no longer stood for the word of God.

Bonhoeffer stated that
"if synagogues burn today the churches will be on fire tomorrow."

TURNING TOWARD THE RESISTANCE

Bonhoeffer already had been displeased with the Confessing Church's cowardly stance in response to the arrest of Werner Koch, the Finkenwalde graduate accused of leaking the memo to Hitler. Heeding the cries of "Treason," the church distanced itself from him and insisted that he had acted on his own. Although the church was eager to dismiss the Koch case, Bonhoeffer and the Finkenwalde community would not abandon their colleague and brother. When Koch was released from a concentration camp in December of 1938, Bonhoeffer arranged a vacation for him in Pomerania so that he could recover his health. Bonhoeffer drove Koch to the appointed destination, and on their long car ride through the countryside he inquired at length about the camp and his friend's experience there. Their conversation was dotted with long interludes of silence, and it occurred to Koch what was happening. "It became clear to me that he was using all his strength to imagine how he himself would behave if he were in the same situation—he was certain that it would happen to him."

By then, Bonhoeffer had ample reason to wonder what went on at concentration camps. His frustration with the church's apathy led him to seek out other means of opposition. Earlier that year his brother-in-law, Hans von Dohnanyi, introduced him to some of the leading members of the German Resistance, including several Army generals and Admiral Canaris, head of the military intelligence organization known as the *Abwehr*. These men were outraged by Hitler and in disbelief that such a maniacal leader could have won the loyalty and respect of their peers in government and their countrymen. Von Dohnanyi, a brave and brilliant man, shared Bonhoeffer's convictions about the Nazis and his willingness to take action. While at the Justice Ministry he had begun keeping a record of the injustices committed by the Nazis, most of which were censored by the Nazi-controlled press or concealed altogether. His hope was that after Hitler was removed from power and the Nazi Party dismantled,

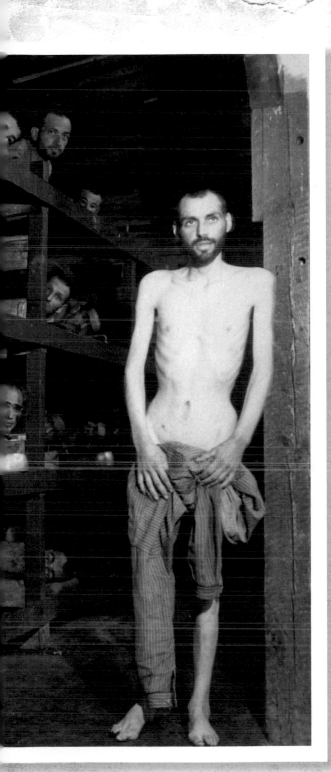

A photo of Jewish slave laborers in the Buchenwald concentration camp on April 16, 1945. Second row, seventh from left is Elie Wiesel, who survived Hitler's death camp to become an internationally acclaimed writer, political activist, and Nobel Peace Prize winner.

the record could be used to prosecute the Nazis for the crimes they had committed. In the meantime he risked his life to share the information and convince others that action was necessary. If the Nazis ever discovered his chronicle, his life was in danger.

By the beginning of 1939, Bonhoeffer had become deeply involved in the Resistance. The Bonhoeffer home in Berlin was an important meeting place where conspirators exchanged information and strategized. Bonhoeffer became closely acquainted with these powerful men, and some even turned to him for spiritual advice. According to Bethge, Bonhoeffer had a unique ability to help people make difficult decisions such as the conspirators were weighing. Von Dohnanyi once asked about the Biblical passage that claimed that those who live by the sword shall die by the sword. Bonhoeffer pointed out that it held true for the conspirators as well, but that the situation in Germany called for people willing to take decisive action, knowing that they might be destroyed in the process.

LEAVING FOR AMERICA, AVOIDING THE DRAFT

In the spring of 1939, Bonhoeffer faced a difficult decision of his own, one that he agonized over for months. War seemed imminent, and men of Bonhoeffer's age would be called up for military service. If he joined the army, he would have to pledge allegiance to Hitler and participate in a war he felt was evil and immoral. If he refused to serve he would be tried before a military tribunal and imprisoned or executed. It was likely that his family might be made to suffer as well, and such a stand would likely do great harm to the Confessing Church. Many Confessing Church pastors had already volunteered for military service to prove their patriotism. The last thing the church needed was for one of its leading members to be accused of cowardice. In a letter to Bishop Bell, Bonhoeffer lamented that he would do "tremendous damage to my brethren" if he was openly hostile to military service.

Yet fighting for Hitler in a war of aggression would go against everything he stood for. This was his predicament.

Hoping that a change of scenery would put his mind at ease and help him resolve the situation, Bonhoeffer traveled to England in early March of 1938. Bethge went with him, and they stayed with Sabine and her family. Bonhoeffer met with contacts from the ecumenical movement and brought them up to date about events inside Germany. Bishop Bell offered his counsel, too. He felt that leaving Germany at that time was not a dishonorable thing to do, nor would it damage the Confessing Church.

There was one possibility. Bonhoeffer might travel back to America and continue his ecumenical work from there for a while. He wrote to his old professor at Union, Reinhold Niebuhr, who happened to be in England at the time giving lectures. He explained his situation and asked for Niebuhr's help. Niebuhr wrote two of his colleagues in New York, one of them being the president of Union Seminary, Henry Sloane Coffin. He also wrote Bonhoeffer's old friend and traveling companion Paul Lehmann, who was teaching in Chicago. Niebuhr's efforts stirred great interest in America, and in the second week of May Bonhoeffer received a letter from Henry Leiper. Leiper headed the Central Bureau of Interchurch Aid and offered Bonhoeffer a position as a pastor to German refugees; he also offered him a lecturing position at Union.

If Bonhoeffer left now, there was a chance that he would be unable to return to Germany under the Third Reich. Yet the Confessing Church was in a harried state, divided on a number of issues and averse to Karl Barth. Still unsure of whether he was doing the right thing, Bonhoeffer booked passage on a ship leaving for New York on June 4. From the moment he stepped ashore in America he could not shake the feeling that he had made a mistake.

CHAPTER NINE

RETURN TO DANGER

Once in New York Bonhoeffer moved into a comfortable apartment at the heart of Union's campus, and within days of his arrival he was relaxing in the rolling Massachusetts countryside with Union president Henry Sloane Coffin. Coffin hosted several parties at his home to make Bonhoeffer feel welcome. Outwardly pleasant and charming as always, on the inside Bonhoeffer was really in agony, tormented by thoughts of the church struggle back home. He could not let go of the feeling that he had abandoned the young theologians whom he had repeatedly encouraged to resist evil. In his diary he wrote, "I do not know why I am here. . . . The short prayer in which we remembered the German brethren almost overwhelmed me. . . . The whole weight of self-reproach because of a wrong decision comes back and almost chokes me." Though safe in New York, he had lost everything that made up his life.

Bonhoeffer spent the first few weeks meditating in prayer, reading, and writing. He was anxious to hear news from Germany, yet none had come. Compounding his internal disquiet was an unexpected feeling of loneliness. He had spent considerable time abroad, and his homesickness perplexed him. It was a new and strange feeling for him. In his diary he also expressed frustration with speaking English, saying that the language hindered his thinking.

He visited several churches and initially was generally disappointed with the status quo of American Christianity. In his diary he wrote scathingly about the service he had attended at the famous Riverside Church (built by Rockefeller), calling it a "respectable, self-indulgent, self-satisfied religious celebration. . . . Perhaps the [Americans] are really more religious than we are, but they are certainly not more Christian." Yet later on the same day he ventured down the street from Union to another church, where he found preaching and community to his liking. In his diary he called the sermon "astonishing" and commented that it "opened up to me an America of which I was quite ignorant before." He compared the clash between two such opposite churches in America with the struggle in Germany and beseeched God to "grant me . . . clarity about my future."

Several days later he made a fateful decision: he would return to Germany on the first available ship. He regretted that his sudden return would disappoint his colleagues in America, who had gone to great lengths to secure his safety there, but his place was in Germany, in what he called the "trenches" of the church struggle there. In a letter to Niebuhr, he explained his decision:

> I have made a mistake in coming to America. I must live through this difficult period of our national history with the Christian people of Germany. I will have no right to participate in the reconstruction of Christian life in Germany after the war if I do not share the trials of this time with my people.

The altar and apse with clerestory windows in
the Riverside Church in New York City

July 7 was Bonhoeffer's last day in New York. Paul Lehmann had come to town to bid his friend farewell. He accompanied Bonhoeffer to the ship, pleading all the while that he change his mind and remain in New York. It was of no use. After the ship pulled away for Europe, Bonhoeffer noted with relief that his inner turmoil had ceased. He never regretted his decision to return to Germany, even when he realized that it had probably cost him his life.

Upon reaching England Bonhoeffer spent ten days visiting his sister and Franz Hildebrandt. Then he slipped back into Germany. Helmut Traub, who had replaced Bonhoeffer at the secret seminary near Schlawe, was stunned to look up one day and see Bonhoeffer standing before him. Traub respectfully chastised Bonhoeffer for returning to such a dangerous situation, especially in light of the tremendous effort that had been made to get him safely out of the country. Bonhoeffer explained that he had made a mistake in going to America, that he was not even sure why he had done it. When students questioned why he would voluntarily return to such a desperate situation he assured them that he had no illusions about the future, stating firmly, "I know what I have chosen."

A few weeks later, Bonhoeffer's parents relayed word from the highest ranks of government that war was about to begin. Bonhoeffer shut down the Schlawe seminary. Once fighting began, his students would be called on to serve.

WAR BEGINS

Germany invaded Poland on September 1, 1939. Hitler knew that he could not invade Poland without a reason, so he fabricated one. SS agents masquerading as Polish soldiers stormed a German radio station on August 31 at the German-Polish border. During the staged attack a Jewish man, dressed as a German soldier, was murdered. Hitler framed the violent break-in as plausible grounds for a declaration of war, and the next day he unleashed the Luftwaffe (air force) into Polish skies while German troops marched below. Civilian casualties mounted with lightning speed. Within a few days Great Britain, France, Australia, and New Zealand declared their solidarity with Poland. World War II began.

Over the next six years, most of the one hundred fifty students who had passed through Finkenwalde, including Eberhard Bethge, would become soldiers on the front lines. At least eighty of them would be killed in action. A few avoided the military by serving in isolated parishes, while others were imprisoned in concentration camps. Bonhoeffer and Bethge spent much of their time writing letters of consolation and encouragement to former students and their families.

September 1939 also marked the beginning of the Nazis's experimentation with mass murder. The extermination schemes they devised were first developed in experiments on German children. Between 1936 and 1939 doctors had been required to register all children born with birth defects. These children interfered with Hitler's plan to develop a "pure" German master race.

The Royal Castle in Warsaw, Poland, burns after being shelled by the Germans in September 1939.

After the invasion of Poland Hitler began ordering churches and state institutions to release the disabled children into the care of the government. State officials would load the children into trucks or vans and take them to remote areas. There, with no witnesses about, the children were killed by lethal injection or poison gas. A day or two later the children's families received a notice saying that their son or daughter had passed away from an illness and that their bodies had already been cremated.

Between 1939 and 1941 the Nazis murdered more than 70,000 children and disabled adults in this fashion. Because so many of the victims came from church hospitals and other charitable institutions, church officials were among the first to realize what was happening. When news of the program finally reached the public, people were shocked—yet they refused to believe their Führer was behind such a heinous campaign. Hitler refuted the allegations and, pretending to heed the public's outcry, ordered a halt to the program. He continued a variation of the program in secret, subjecting disabled persons to experimental medical treatments. Many of them died during treatment or from forced starvation, yet they served their purpose. The results of these experiments were used in developing a highly sophisticated system of mass murder that eventually claimed the lives of millions.

THE DOUBLE AGENT: JOINING THE RESISTANCE

Bonhoeffer followed these developments closely. The church was responding feebly to this unimaginable evil, leading him to consider other ways to channel his opposition. "Mere waiting and looking on," he once wrote, "is not Christian behavior. The Christian is called to sympathy and action, not in the first place by his own suffering, but by the sufferings of his brethren, for whose sake Christ suffered." Before he had left for America, Bonhoeffer met with a small group of friends to tell them about his decision to go to New York. At one point in their conversation he had asked whether they would absolve a man complicit in the murder of a despot. Aside from Bethge, none of his friends were aware of his involvement with the Resistance; they did not suspect that his question had a personal undertone. Now, having chosen to return to the "trenches" in Germany, Bonhoeffer was ready to take serious action—more than the Confessing Church had in mind.

He began spending more and more time with the conspirators who were plotting Hitler's overthrow. Admiral Canaris and von Dohnanyi used their influence to secure Bonhoeffer a position in the Abwehr. As a state official he was exempt from military service and did not have to swear allegiance to Hitler. In theory, Bonhoeffer's status as a pastor and his frequent international travel for ecumenical work made him the perfect spy. No one would suspect that he was gathering intelligence for the Nazis. In reality, Bonhoeffer was a double agent. Although he provided the Abwehr with reports on the ecumenical movement, his real mission was to let international leaders know that there was a resistance movement inside of Germany in need of support.

Now leading a double life, Bonhoeffer's behavior puzzled many in the Confessing Church. It seemed to them as though he really had gone over to the side of the Nazis. He could not answer their questions, for fear of risking the lives of those in the Resistance, and his reputation as an honest and straightforward man suffered. By this time, though, he was not caught up on what other people thought.

On June 17, 1940, he and Bethge were sitting at an outdoor cafe in Memel when news came over a loudspeaker that France had just surrendered. Fellow Germans, overcome with joy, began dancing, singing, and shouting "Germany, Germany above all!" To Bethge's amazement Bonhoeffer, who in the past had refused to even make the regulation Hitler salute, now stood and triumphantly raised his arm with the others. "Raise your arm! Are you crazy?" he whispered sharply to Bethge. Afterward he explained, "We shall have to run risks for very different things now, but not for that salute!"

German soldiers marching past the Arc de Triomphe
after the surrender of Paris in June 1940

The fall of France and the surrender of Belgium and Holland were huge setbacks for the Resistance. With these victories the entire nation seemed to be in awe of the Führer's military genius, and churches held joyous thanksgiving services to celebrate. Most everyone believed that the words written on the belt buckle of each German soldier—"God with us!"—were true. This was the case in the Confessing Church, too, and Bonhoeffer realized he would have to carry out his duties for the Resistance without the Church's knowledge or approval. Even the most radical among the Church's leadership would likely regard a conspiracy to overthrow Hitler as treasonous. No one in the Confessing Church—except his friend Eberhard Bethge—could know of his double life.

Bonhoeffer met Barth for what would be the last time in 1941. Part of his Abwehr service involved traveling to neutral Switzerland several times that year to meet with church leaders. At the border this time he was required to submit the name of a Swiss citizen who could vouch for him. He named Karl Barth. Barth gave his permission but was suspicious. He assumed that the only way a Confessing Church pastor could get permission to travel during wartime was if he supported Hitler. When the two men met, Bonhoeffer revealed his double-agent status, though Barth remained somewhat suspicious of his younger friend's involvement with the Abwehr. While in Switzerland Bonhoeffer visited his old friend Erwin Sutz, too. He also took the opportunity to write long letters to Sabine and Bishop Bell in England. Being in a country where he could communicate freely again boosted his spirits. In Geneva he stayed with Adolf Freudenberg, a man he had met while working in the ecumenical movement.

From 1941 until 1943 Bonhoeffer was constantly on the move, traveling around Germany and outside of the country, too. Munich, Berlin, the Bonhoeffer summer home in Friedrichsbrunn, and a Catholic monastery in Ettal were some of the places he stayed during that period. During interludes between traveling he began work on a new book that addressed the question of how Christians should respond to tyrannical regimes like Hitler's. He argued that churches that vowed to stay neutral in the face of blatant inhumanity were not neutral at all—their inaction actually encouraged injustice and oppression. Tolerating a regime that murdered millions of innocent people was worse than trying to overthrow its leader by violent force.

This thinking formed the basis of Bonhoeffer's writing that became *Ethics* and *Letters and Papers from Prison*. His whole life he had been consumed with the notion of responsibility. He saw his calling as coming not from himself, from the state, or even from the church, but fundamentally from God, to whom his ultimate allegiance was. "The ultimately responsible question is not how I extricate myself heroically from a situation," he concluded, "but [how] a coming generation is to go on living." It was with this view of a responsibility to mankind and the future, through allegiance to God, that he joined the Resistance and became a double agent.

THE "FINAL SOLUTION TO THE JEWISH QUESTION"

By September 1941 the situation for Germany's Jews had became extremely desperate. First they were required to wear a yellow star on their clothing, and by October their forcible removal to concentration camps began. In January of 1942, party officials and SS officers met at a Berlin estate on the Wannsee to plan "The Final Solution to the Jewish Question." General Heydrich had devised a plan to deport all the remaining Jews in Germany and Europe to special death camps in Germany. At the camps large-scale murder of the prisoners would be carried out with factory-like efficiency.

Just before the Wannsee Conference Bonhoeffer had been involved in his most serious counterespionage scheme of yet, called Operation 7. It involved delicate and dangerous bureaucratic maneuvering to get a group of Jews safely out of Germany. Admiral Canaris and von Dohnanyi wanted to help some of their friends escape deportation. First they had to be taken off the deportation lists, then made agents of Abwehr. This had to be done without arousing suspicion with the Gestapo. The last and most complicated hurdle was convincing Swiss officials to accept them. Switzerland maintained neutrality in the war and did not help German Jews. Bonhoeffer eventually got permission by appealing to Swiss church officials he had worked with in the ecumenical movement, but the offer came with a price. Their plan succeeded, but not without the Gestapo noticing the trail of foreign currency that the Abwehr paid the Swiss. That blip on the Nazi radar eventually came to expose the Resistance.

As part of another Abwehr mission Bonhoeffer traveled to Sweden in 1942. There he met with Bishop Bell and briefed him on the Resistance. It was the first time that the two had seen each other since Bonhoeffer's departure to New York in 1939, and Bonhoeffer was especially glad to see him because he brought good word of Sabine and her family. As for Abwehr business, the hope was that Bell would be able to convince leaders in the British government and its allies to provide the Resistance a guarantee of support should they act to remove Hitler. Unfortunately, Bell never was able to persuade British leaders to take that step. Nevertheless, Bonhoeffer was immensely grateful to talk with his dear friend for what he suspected might be the last time. Later, he wrote Bell, thanking him for his generosity and time. "This spirit of fellowship and of Christian brotherliness will carry me through the darkest hour, and even if things go worse than we hope and expect, the light of these few days will never extinguish in my heart."

CHAPTER TEN

ARREST AND MARTYRDOM

England's refusal to come to the side of the conspirators did not deter them from going ahead with their plot to assassinate Hitler. Bonhoeffer was not directly involved in carrying out the mission, but his complicity in the plot was an offense punishable by death. The conspirators had no illusions about the grave consequences of failure, and tensions were high as the planned date drew nearer. In his Christmas letter of 1942—the last Christmas he would spend as a free man—Bonhoeffer wrote of the difficulties of "living every day as if it were our last, and yet living in faith and responsibility as though there were to be a great future." Yet in a move that astonished his friends and family, Bonhoeffer made a very personal commitment to the future: he became engaged to a young woman named Maria von Wedemeyer.

Bonhoeffer had often insisted that his hectic life made marriage impossible. In the mid-1930s he had broken off a serious relationship because of his academic and pastoral posts abroad, as well as his regular traveling for the ecumenical movement and responsibilities to the Confessing Church. Maria von Wedemeyer, however, was a most unusual young woman and intrigued Bonhoeffer from their first meeting. Although she was only eighteen years old in 1943, roughly half his age, she was confident enough to challenge him intellectually. Her grandmother, Ruth von Kleist-Restow, was a generous supporter of the Confessing Church movement, and Bonhoeffer had been a frequent guest at the von Wedemeyer family estate in Pomerania. It was there, after a trip in 1942 to meet with members of the Italian Resistance, that he really noticed Maria.

They subsequently met several times in Berlin, where Maria was visiting her grandmother in surgery, and Bonhoeffer realized that he had fallen in love with her. Maria's father had recently died, so Bonhoeffer asked her mother to bless the engagement. Maria's family was reluctant to give their daughter away on account of her youth, as well as for their inkling about Bonhoeffer's underground activities. Partially through the encouragement of Maria's grandmother, who admired Bonhoeffer, a one-year engagement was agreed upon.

TRYING TO ASSASSINATE HITLER

By early 1943 the assassination plot had acquired an enormous urgency. Through their connections with the innermost circles of Nazi leadership, the Resistance knew of the grisly crimes being committed at the death camps. And plans were in place to murder millions more Jews there. Meanwhile, Russian troops had steadily been crushing German armies on the Eastern Front, a setback that made the Nazis vulnerable. It was time to act.

In March 1943 von Dohnanyi, General Oster, and Admiral Canaris were at the Eastern Front for a military intelligence meeting. The trio had brought explosives with them, and after the meeting they smuggled a time bomb onto Hitler's plane that was set to explode after take-off. Back in Berlin, Bonhoeffer and his family waited anxiously for word of the plot's success. It never came. Cold temperatures in the cargo hold had likely caused the time mechanism to malfunction. Fortunately, the conspirators dodged discovery by sneaking aboard the plane after it landed and removing the bomb.

A week later, on March 21, another attempt was made on the Führer's life. He was scheduled to tour an army museum. Rudolph von Gersdorff, the young officer selected to serve as Hitler's guide through the exhibitions, volunteered to sacrifice his life in order to end Hitler's. With two bombs hidden in his pockets, he was to stand beside the Führer and detonate the explosives. But this second attempt, too, was foiled; a sudden change of plans prompted Hitler to rush with haste through the museum and leave only a few minutes after entering. Although von Gersdorff managed to light the fuse of one bomb, Hitler left before it detonated. Fortunately, von Gersdorff was able to duck into a nearby rest room to extinguish the fuse and escape discovery.

The failure of these two assassination attempts was disastrous for the conspirators. Time was running out, and the Gestapo had already begun following the foreign currency trail from Operation 7. They were connecting dots that led straight to Bonhoeffer, and they had already nabbed Abwehr member Wilhelm Schmidhuber, who would concede the names of his co-conspirators.

ARREST AND IMPRISONMENT

Around noon on April 5, Bonhoeffer called the von Dohnanyi home to talk with his sister, Christine. When a strange voice answered the phone he guessed that Christine and her husband had been arrested and the Gestapo was probably searching their house for incriminating evidence. After checking his room to make sure nothing was there to arouse suspicion, he went next door to his sister Ursula's house, asked her to fix him a big meal, and then quietly waited. The moment he feared had come at last. Bonhoeffer had once written that, although he was not eager to go to prison, if it came to that he hoped he could do so with joy since their cause was worthy. Around four o'clock that afternoon the Gestapo located Bonhoeffer. A few minutes later he was escorted to a black Mercedes, Bible in hand, and driven off. His family never saw him outside of prison again.

Bonhoeffer was taken to Tegel, a military prison northwest of Berlin. Although he had often visited former Finkenwalde students in prison, the brutality and callousness of Tegel that first night still shocked him. The blankets he was given had such a foul odor that he could not bear to use them. And a weeping prisoner in the cell adjoining his kept him awake all night. His breakfast next morning was a stale piece of bread thrown on the floor. For twelve long days Bonhoeffer was held in solitary confinement, hearing only the screams and cries of other prisoners being abused by interrogators. No one was allowed to speak with him.

Bonhoeffer in the courtyard of Tegel prison in the summer of 1944

Assuming he was about to be executed, Bonhoeffer considered suicide, "not from a sense of guilt, but because basically I am already dead." His fate was not yet so certain. Although the Gestapo suspected an Abwehr conspiracy they had no proof. Fortunately, Bonhoeffer and von Dohnanyi had worked out complicated but plausible cover stories beforehand. He was questioned extensively—particularly about Operation 7—but Bonhoeffer convincingly played the part of an innocent, naive pastor who had simply been trying to help his country.

Whether he would hold up under torture was his greatest worry. To his relief, he was not tortured, perhaps because his cousin, General Paul von Hase, was the military commandant of Berlin. After the first twelve days, conditions for Bonhoeffer improved markedly. He was allowed books and writing paper, as well as contact with other prisoners and guards. Because his family was allowed to send him books they communicated with him through the use of a secret code they had worked out ahead of time. If his name was underlined on the inside cover it meant that, starting from the back of the book, he would find a faint pencil mark placed under a letter every two pages. The letters spelled out messages from the family. When Bonhoeffer returned books, he used the same code. Von Dohnanyi was also allowed books, and the family relayed information between the two. That proved a tremendous help in keeping their stories straight. In the end, frustrated interrogators could get neither Bonhoeffer nor von Dohnanyi to change their cover stories.

WAITING, WRITING, PRAYING

After the first few weeks, Bonhoeffer settled in for a long and nerve-wracking period of waiting. His trial was postponed numerous times. Being a man of action, he found these delays severely frustrating. Still, he was able to mitigate his frustration with a regular routine of study, meditation, prayer, exercise, and writing. His caring personality won over both prisoners and guards, and he was granted permission to move about the prison.

In the evenings he even helped out in the infirmary. Friendly guards arranged illegal, unsupervised visits with his family and smuggled his letters out of prison. That allowed him to bypass censoring and establish communication with Eberhard Bethge. His correspondence with Bethge would form the book *Letters and Papers from Prison*.

By the fall of 1943 Bonhoeffer was engrossed in developing a new theology based on what he called "religionless Christianity" and a "world come of age." He devoted great energy to writing about these new concepts, and gradually, his impatience with prison life waned. He accepted that, in sharing the suffering of those at Tegel, he was where Christ wanted him to be. "It is not the religious act that makes the Christian," he wrote, "but participation in the sufferings of God in the secular life. . . . Jesus calls men, not to a new religion, but to life." In a letter to Bethge he wrote how he had once thought he could acquire faith by trying to live a holy life. "I discovered later, and I'm still discovering right up to this moment," he marveled, "that it is only by living completely in this world that one learns to have faith."

Harold Poelchau, the prison's chaplain, recalled that at this point Bonhoeffer was so trusted and moved about the prison so freely that escape would have been easy. Bonhoeffer resisted the urge to leave, because he did not want to endanger his family or whoever might give him refuge. Outwardly at ease, Bonhoeffer had private moments of despair. A poem he composed in June of 1944 illustrates his inner unrest:

> Who am I? They often tell me
> I would step from my cell's confinement
> calmly, cheerfully, firmly,
> like a squire from his country-house.
>
> Who am I? They often tell me
> I would talk to my warders
> freely and friendly and clearly,
> as though it were mine to command.

Who am I? They also tell me
I would bear the days of misfortune
equably, smilingly, proudly,
like one accustomed to win.

Am I then really all that which other men tell of?
Or am I only what I know of myself,
restless and longing and sick, like a bird in a cage,
struggling for breath, as though hands were
   compressing my throat,
yearning for colors, for flowers, for the voices of birds,
thirsting for words of kindness, for neighbourliness
trembling with anger at despotisms and petty humiliation,
tossing in expectation of great events,
powerlessly trembling for friends at an infinite distance,
weary and empty at praying, at thinking, at making,
faint, and ready to say farewell to all?

Bonhoeffer's unshakable faith shone forth in the poem's last line—"Whoever I am, Thou knowest, O God, I am thine." In the past Bonhoeffer had kept his feelings bottled up inside. Expressing himself in poetry was something that owed much to Maria's influence. In her visits and letters she encouraged him to drop the mask of competence he so often presented to the world and express what he really felt. The restrictions of prison were causing the man some people regarded as a saint to become more human. His letters to Maria touched on topics that any couple engaged to be married might discuss: details of their wedding, how they would raise their children or decorate their home.

THE JULY 20 PLOT

On July 20, 1944, another assassination attempt was set to take place. Bonhoeffer, von Dohnanyi, and the other imprisoned con-spirators were keenly aware of the plan, and if it succeeded they might soon be free men. Colonel Claus von Stauffenberg had volunteered to carry a briefcase containing a bomb into a conference room where Hitler was meeting with other military leaders. Von Stauffenberg placed the briefcase near Hitler's chair and then quietly walked away. But at the last moment another officer moved the briefcase. Moments later, a powerful blast rocked the room, killing four officers and severely injuring two others. Miraculously, Hitler survived the explosion with only cuts, bruises, and broken eardrums. He immediately set about seeking revenge. By midnight von Stauffenberg had been found and shot. Two hundred others would be executed in the next few months, often in the most cruel and humiliating ways possible— Hitler even had some of their deaths filmed for his enjoyment.

Bonhoeffer heard the distressing news of Hitler's survival over the prison radio and guessed that it was only a matter of time before he was linked indisputably to the conspiracy. He immediately wrote Bethge a letter that ended with a prayer: "May God in his mercy lead us through these times; but above all, may he lead us to himself." The Gestapo did not immediately identify his connection to the plot. But then the Gestapo found a copy of von Dohnanyi's chronicle, the one in which he had catalogued Nazi injustices in great detail. Members of the Resistance thought it had been destroyed, but General Beck had kept a copy. It contained the names of most of those involved in the conspiracy, and the Gestapo now had a hit list.

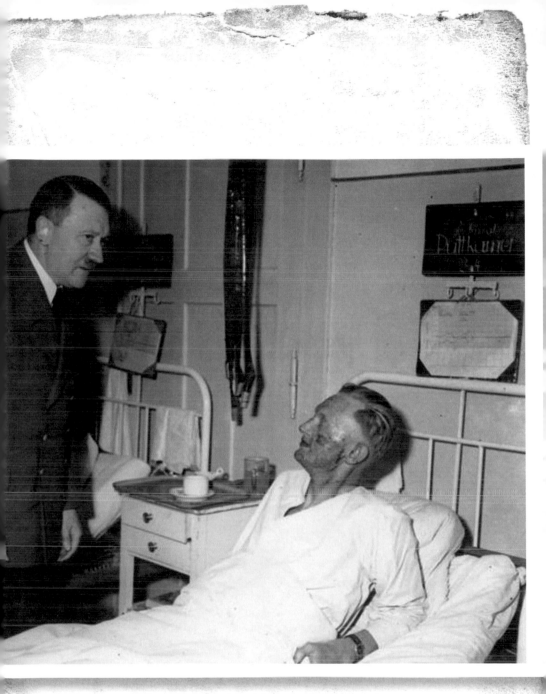

Hitler visits Admiral Karl-Jesco von Puttkamer, who was
wounded in the July 20 assassination attempt.

Bonhoeffer's family organized one last attempt to free him through escape. Corporal Knobloch, a friendly guard, volunteered to sneak Bonhoeffer out of prison and hide him in a safe place. Bonhoeffer's sister Ursula and her husband Rudiger Schleicher even met with Knobloch to give him a mechanic's uniform to use as a disguise. The escape was set for early October, but on October 1, Bonhoeffer's brother Klaus was arrested. For Bonhoeffer, that changed everything. He abandoned the plan, believing that an escape would only cause more problems for Maria and his family.

A MOVE FOR THE WORSE

A week later guards moved Bonhoeffer to Gestapo headquarters at Prinz Albrecht Strasse, a grim and hopeless prison notorious for torture and brutality. There is no evidence that Bonhoeffer was tortured there, but most inmates were. During his four months there no one from his family was permitted to talk with him, and he wrote only three brief letters. Recollections of fellow prisoners provide brief glimpses of his final few months of life. Fabian von Schlabrendorff, a cousin of Maria's, was one of those prisoners—the Gestapo was now arresting everyone remotely connected to the conspirators.

Schlabrendorff was amazed at Bonhoeffer's even-tempered nature. He was so kind and polite to everyone that guards, too, were won over. They even apologized to him when they had to lock his cell after he returned from the exercise yard. When he received letters from Maria or his family, his eyes shone with feeling as he told Schlabrendorff that he felt their love near him. On Wednesdays they sent him packages of food. Without fail he would share what he had received. "It delighted him that even in prison you were able to help your neighbor, and let him share in what you had," recalled Schlabrendorff.

Although much of his time was spent alone in his cell he got the chance to visit with other prisoners during the air raids that occurred almost nightly. Whenever Allied bombers flew over the city, prisoners were herded into a shelter in the prison yard. Like many inmates, Schlabrendorff sometimes lost hope, but he recalled that Bonhoeffer was always able to cheer him up and comfort him. "He never tired of repeating," Schlabrendorff remembered, "that the only fight which is lost is that which we give up."

Bonhoeffer took his own advice to heart. When he learned that von Dohnanyi, now paralyzed in both legs, was also at Prinz Albrecht Strasse, he made a bold and dangerous move. As he and the other prisoners filed toward the air raid shelter one night, Bonhoeffer suddenly dived into von Dohnanyi's open cell. Miraculously, no one saw him. During the air raid he and von Dohnanyi compared notes on their interrogations and agreed on future testimony. When the raid was over, Bonhoeffer somehow blended back into the line of prisoners without being discovered. If they could only hold out until the war ended, he and Maria might yet be married.

During the night of February 3, 1945, Allied bombers turned much of Berlin into rubble. The prison was hit and the air raid shelter rocked. A few days later Bonhoeffer and about twenty other men were loaded into trucks and moved to the Buchenwald concentration camp near Weimar, almost two hundred miles south of Berlin. He spent the next two months in the basement of an SS barracks just outside the main camp. Most of the inmates with Bonhoeffer were political prisoners. Also among them was Payne Best, a captured British officer who arrived at Buchenwald two weeks after Bonhoeffer. Best remembered that Bonhoeffer "was different; just quite calm and normal, seemingly perfectly at his ease . . . his soul really shone in the dark desperation of our prison."

The prisoners' moods alternated between great hope and utter fear. The war was nearly over, but important prisoners were supposed to be marched into the woods and shot if the enemy approached a concentration camp. On April 1, prisoners at Buchenwald heard American artillery in the distance. Two days later Bonhoeffer and several other prisoners, including

Payne Best, were loaded into a van and driven southeast away from the camp. They were headed toward the death camp at Flossenbürg, and it took the slow-moving van almost a week to get there.

April 8 was a Sunday. Bonhoeffer was with a group of prisoners in a schoolhouse in the village of Schönberg. Generous villagers had given the prisoners food, and someone asked Bonhoeffer to lead a service of thanksgiving. At first he refused—he did not want to offend anyone. But when everyone spoke in favor, he agreed. According to officer Best, Bonhoeffer found just the right words to touch their hearts as they looked hopefully toward the future.

Moments after the service ended, two armed men appeared in the doorway. "Prisoner Bonhoeffer," they announced, "take your things and come with us." Everyone knew that he was being led away to his death. Given a few moments to collect his belongings, Bonhoeffer had time to whisper his last words to Best. It was a message to Bishop Bell: "Tell him that for me this is the end, but also the beginning."

From Schönberg, Bonhoeffer was driven the short distance to Flossenbürg concentration camp. That night he and five other conspirators, including General Oster and Admiral Canaris, were put on trial and interrogated one last time. At six in the morning on April 9, they were taken from their cells and read the guilty verdict. They were led down a flight of steps to the secluded place of execution. Bonhoeffer said a short prayer before his life was ended.

Execution site at prison camp near Nuremburg where
theologian Dietrich Bonhoeffer died in 1944

EPILOGUE

LEGACY

Had Hitler's final wishes regarding Eberhard Bethge been carried out, Dietrich Bonhoeffer's name today might be no more than an obscure historical footnote. In April 1945 only a small number of people inside Germany knew much about his life. Fortunately, Bethge, the man who knew him better than anyone, narrowly escaped death. Hitler would commit suicide before the month ended, but not before personally ordering the execution of several other members of the Bonhoeffer family: Bonhoeffer's brother Klaus and Bonhoeffer's brothers-in-law Hans von Dohnanyi and Rudiger Schleicher. By then, Bethge was also part of the Bonhoeffer family. In April of 1944 he had married Dietrich's niece, Renate Schleicher. Bethge's close association with Bonhoeffer marked him for death, too, but Berlin fell to enemy troops before German officials could execute his sentence.

After the war, Bethge felt obligated to share his friend's final theological ideas—ideas that Bonhoeffer had been particularly excited about. Working from the letters sent him from prison and his understanding of Bonhoeffer's thinking, Bethge published Bonhoeffer's *Ethics* in 1949. But it was the release of *Letters and Papers from Prison* in 1953 that first attracted worldwide attention to Bonhoeffer's life and work. Originally published in German, the book has since been translated into more than fifteen languages. In the decades since his death, dozens of other authors have written books on Bonhoeffer and his theology, and at least five films have been made about his life.

Encouraged by the response to *Letters and Papers*, Bethge devoted the remainder of his life to sharing Bonhoeffer's theology and story. He edited a number of other works written and inspired by his friend, including the sixteen-volume *Collected Works*. His last contribution, *Dietrich Bonhoeffer: A Biography*, was published a few months before Bethge died in 2000.

A statue of Bonhoeffer stands above the Great West Door of Westminster Abbey in London. Along with men like Dr. Martin Luther King and Archbishop Oscar Romero of El Salvador, he is one of ten twentieth-century martyrs depicted there.

Timeline

1906	Born on February 4 in Breslau, Germany.
1912	Moves with family to Berlin where father is professor at the University of Berlin.
1914	World War I begins.
1918	Brother Walter is killed in the war; first considers becoming a theologian; war ends in November with Germany's defeat.
1920	Announces to family his intention to become a theologian.
1923	Enrolls at the University of Tübingen.
1924	Suffers a concussion while ice-skating; visits Italy and North Africa with brother Klaus.
1927	Completes doctoral dissertation, "The Communion of Saints."
1928	Serves one year as assistant pastor at a German congregation in Barcelona, Spain.
1929	Begins lecturing in theology at the University of Berlin.
1930	Completes Habilitation, "Act and Being"; travels to New York to study at Union Seminary.
1931	Travels to Mexico; returns to Germany and meets Karl Barth; lectures in theology at the University of Berlin; becomes youth secretary for the World Alliance of Churches; ordained as a minister; begins teaching confirmation classes at Zionskirche.
1932	Graduates his first confirmation class.
1933	Resists the German Christians after Hitler becomes chancellor; writes Bethel Confession; moves to London to pastor two German congregations.
1934	Implores churches to unite against war at ecumenical conference in Fanø, Denmark; envisions establishing German seminaries modeled on English monasteries.
1935	Inaugurates Finkenwalde seminary, serving as director; establishes the House of Brethren.
1936	Banned from teaching at the University of Berlin; sneaks his seminary students out of the country for a trip to Sweden and Denmark; gives last talk before a large public audience during the Berlin Olympics.

1937	Nazis shut down Finkenwalde; Bonhoeffer publishes *The Cost of Discipleship*; teaches at secret seminaries in Köslin and Gross-Schlönwitz.
1938	Forbidden to work in Berlin; helps Sabine and her family escape to England; writes *Life Together*.
1939	Visits London and discusses his future with Bishop Bell; leaves for the United States in June, but quickly returns to Germany; joins the Abwehr as a civilian agent.
1940	Nazis shut down seminaries in Köslin and Gross-Schlönwitz; Bonhoeffer begins writing *Ethics*.
1941	Carries out Operation 7, Abwehr mission to help Jews escape to Switzerland.
1942	Travels to Norway and Sweden on counterespionage mission to encourage Allied support of German Resistance.
1943	Becomes engaged to Maria von Wedemeyer; arrested and imprisoned at Tegel Prison; begins secret correspondence with family and Eberhard Bethge.
1944	Valkyrie assassination on Hitler fails; Gestapo uncovers evidence implicating Resistance conspirators; refuses to escape from Tegel Prison for fear of endangering others; moved to prison at Gestapo headquarters.
1945	Shipped to Buchenwald concentration camp; sentenced to death at Flossenbürg concentration camp; hanged on April 9 with five other Resistance conspirators; Hitler commits suicide.

Sources

CHAPTER ONE: *Man of Action*

p. 9, "In the almost fifty years . . ." Eberhard Bethge, *Dietrich Bonhoeffer: A Biography* (Minneapolis: Fortress Press, 2000), 928.

p. 12, "there was little difficulty . . ." Mary Bosanquet, *The Life and Death of Dietrich Bonhoeffer* (London: Hodder and Stoughton, 1968), 29.

p. 13, "While we were playing . . ." Wolf-Dieter Zimmerman and Ronald G. Smith, eds., *I Knew Dietrich Bonhoeffer*, trans. Käthe G. Smith (New York: Harper and Row, 1966), 24.

p. 15, "Only space will divide us!" Bosanquet, *Life and Death*, 35.

p. 15, "In that case . . ." Bethge, *A Biography*, 36.

CHAPTER TWO: *A Theological Rebel*

p. 19, "Everyone who knew him . . ." Bethge, *A Biography*, 42.

p. 20, "too narrow for his spirit," Zimmerman and Smith, *I Knew Dietrich Bonhoeffer*, 33.

p. 20, "You may chop off . . ." Edwin Robertson, *The Shame and the Sacrifice: The Life and Martyrdom of Dietrich Bonhoeffer* (New York: Macmillan Publishing Company, 1988), 36.

p. 21, "In nearly every field . . ." Bethge, *A Biography*, 50.

p. 23, "white, black, yellow faces . . ." Bosanquet, *Life and Death*, 52.

p. 26, "free, critical and independent . . ." Elizabeth Raum, *Dietrich Bonhoeffer: Called by God* (New York: Continuum, 2002), 34.

p. 27, "If you want to find God . . ." Bosanquet, *Life and Death*, 72.

p. 27, "Christianity means decision . . ." Robertson, *Shame and Sacrifice*, 45.

p. 29, "This offer seemed to bring to fruition . . ." Dietrich Bonhoeffer, *Dietrich Bonhoeffer Works*, ed. Clifford J. Green, trans. Doublas W. Stott (New York: Fortress Press, 2008), 10:57.

CHAPTER THREE: *Barcelona and New York*

p. 33, "What this will is . . ." Bosanquet, *Life and Death*, 74.

p. 35, "In your place I should . . ." Raum, *Called by God*, 43.

p. 38, "one of the most pleasing and significant events . . ." Ibid., 47.

p. 38, "His impressive physique . . ." Zimmerman, *I Knew Dietrich Bonhoeffer*, 42.

p. 39, "quite simply," Renate Wind, *Dietrich Bonhoeffer: A Spoke in the Wheel* (Grand Rapids, MI: William B. Eerdmans Publishing Company, 1992), 53.

p. 41, "He had an extraordinarily even . . ." Robertson, *Shame and Sacrifice*, 66.

p. 41, "I was quite pleased with myself . . ." Dietrich Bonhoeffer, *A Testament to Freedom*, ed. Geffrey B. Kelly and F. Burton Nelson (San Francisco: HarperSanFrancisco, 1990), 448.

CHAPTER FOUR: *Pastor, Teacher, and Ecumenist*

p. 43, "outlook is really exceptionally grim . . ." Bonhoeffer, *A Testament to Freedom*, 384.

p. 46, "I have been impressed . . ." Bethge, *A Biography*, 176.

p. 47, "I see hardly any of the professors . . ." Bonhoeffer, *A Testament to Freedom*, 384.

p. 49,	"stay[ing] out of curiosity . . ." Zimmerman, *I Knew Dietrich Bonhoeffer*, 60-61.
p. 49,	[Bonhoeffer] pointed out . . ." Ibid.
p. 50,	"followed his words with such close attention . . ." Ibid., 68.
p. 50,	"What was far more important for us . . ." Ibid., 61.
p. 51,	"Bon! Bon! Bon!" Bosanquet, *Life and Death*, 103.
p. 51,	"I have based the entire class . . ." Bethge, *A Biography*, 227.

CHAPTER FIVE: *Battling for the Soul of the Church*

p. 55,	"Our Protestant church . . ." Bosanquet, *Life and Death*, 107.
p. 56,	"leaders or offices which set . . ." Raum, *Called by God*, 59.
p. 57,	"the protection of people . . ." Wind, *A Spoke in the Wheel*, 67.
p. 59,	"Better an ending by terror . . ." George Victor, *Hitler: The Pathology of Evil* (London: Brassey's, 1998), 100.
p. 60,	"When the life or death . . ." Wind, *A Spoke in the Wheel*, 68.
p. 60,	"has no right to [seize] . . ." Ibid., 69.
p. 60,	"The third possibility . . ." Bonhoeffer, *A Testament to Freedom*, 139.
p. 62,	"Keep your race pure!" Wind, *A Spoke in the Wheel*, 71.
p. 63,	"feel deeply thankful that the state . . ." Bethge, *A Biography*, 290.
p. 66,	"The question is really . . ." Eric Metaxas, *Bonhoeffer: Pastor, Martyr, Prophet, Spy* (Nashville, Thomas Nelson Press, 2010), 183.
p. 67,	"I find myself in radical opposition . . ." Bethge, *A Biography*, 325-26.

CHAPTER SIX: *London and Finkenwalde*

p. 70,	"an abundance of humor," Zimmerman, *I Knew Dietrich Bonhoeffer*, 81.
p. 70,	"small and unimportant details . . ." Ibid.
p. 70,	"the house of [Germany's] church . . ." Dietrich Bonhoeffer, *Dietrich Bonhoeffer Works*, ed. Keith Clements, trans. Isabel Best (New York: Fortress Press, 2007), 13:41.
p. 73,	"But we too as Christians . . ." Raum, *Called by God*, 83.
p. 74,	"breathless with tension," Zimmerman, *I Knew Dietrich Bonhoeffer*, 90.
p. 74,	"The hour is late . . ." Deitricht Bonhoeffer, *No Rusty Swords*, ed. Edwin Robertson (New York: Harper & Row, 1965), 291-92.
p. 76,	"the next generation of pastors . . ." Bonhoeffer, *Dietrich Bonhoeffer Works*, 13:217.
p. 76,	"I don't want to leave . . ." Wind, *A Spoke in the Wheel*, 98.
p. 77,	"Most of us were almost . . ." Raum, *Called by God*, 88.
pp. 77-78,	"always felt slightly embarrassed . . ." Zimmerman, *I Knew Dietrich Bonhoeffer*, 126.
pp. 78-79,	"I have been under the spell . . ." Ibid., 126.
p. 80,	"it was a great surprise . . ." Ibid., 109.
p. 81,	"We can give you no . . ." Bethge, *A Biography*, 498.

CHAPTER SEVEN: *Persecution*

p. 83,	"Church and un-church . . ." Zimmerman, *I Knew Dietrich Bonhoeffer*, 129.
p. 83,	"If you board the wrong train . . ." Ibid., 129.
p. 84,	"Take us aboard . . ." Bosanquet, *Life and Death*, 174.
p. 85,	"Whoever knowingly cuts himself off . . ." Bonhoeffer, *A Testament to Freedom*, 173.

p. 89,   "After the Olympiad . . ." Bosanquet, *Life and Death*, 178.

p. 90,   "cheap grace . . ." Dietrich Bonhoeffer, *The Cost of Discipleship* (New York: The Macmillan Company, 1961), 45.

CHAPTER EIGHT: *Secret Lives*

p. 96,   "I arrived here yesterday . . ." Bethge, *A Biography*, 591-92.

p. 96,   "Instead of the stuffy atmosphere . . ." Ibid., 592-93.

p. 98,   "strong and confident . . ." Raum, *Called by God*, 105.

p. 100,   "they burned all the meeting places . . ." Robertson, *Shame and Sacrifice*, 158.

p. 100,   "If the synagogues burn . . ." Zimmerman, *I Knew Dietrich Bonhoeffer*, 150.

p. 100,   "On November 10 . . ." Daniel Jonas Goldhagen, *Hitler's Willing Executioners: Ordinary Germans and the Holocaust* (New York: Vintage, 1997), 111.

p. 101,   "It became clear to me . . ." Wind, *A Spoke in the Wheel*, 123.

p. 104,   "tremendous damage . . ." Raum, *Called by God*, 114.

CHAPTER NINE: *Return to Danger*

p. 107,   "I do not know why I am here . . ." Wind, *A Spoke in the Wheel*, 133.

p. 108,   "respectable, self-indulgent, self-satisfied . . ." Dietrich Bonhoeffer, *Collected Works of Dietrich Bonhoeffer*, ed. Edwin H. Robertson, trans. Edwin H. Robertson and John Bowden (New York: Harper and Row, 1966), 2:230-31.

p. 108,   "astonishing . . ." Metaxas, *Bonhoeffer*, 334.

p. 108,   "trenches," Metaxas, *Bonhoeffer*, 341.

p. 108,   "I have made a mistake . . ." Bethge, *A Biography*, 655.

p. 109,   "I know what I have chosen," Raum, *Called by God*, 116.

p. 112,   "Mere waiting and looking . . ." Bonhoeffer, *A Testament to Freedom*, 508.

p. 113,   "Germany, Germany over all!" Bethge, *A Biography*, 681.

p. 113,   "Raise your arm!" Ibid.

p. 115,   "God with us!" Wind, *A Spoke in the Wheel*, 141.

p. 116,   "The ultimately responsible question . . ." Bonhoeffer, *Letters and Papers from Prison*, ed. Eberhard Bethge (Minneapolis: Fortress, 2010), 42.

p. 117,   "This spirit of fellowship . . ." Bethge, *A Biography*, 762-63.

CHAPTER TEN: *Arrest and Martyrdom*

p. 119,   "living every day . . ." Dietrich Bonhoeffer, *Letters and Papers from Prison*, ed. Eberhard Bethge (New York: Simon & Schuster, 1971), 15.

p. 123,   "not from a sense of guilt . . ." Raum, *Called by God*, 136.

p. 124,   "religionless Christianity," Stephen Plant, *Bonhoeffer* (New York: Continuum, 2004), 134.

p. 124,   "It is not the religious act that makes the Christian . . ." Bonhoeffer, *Letters and Papers*, 361-62.

p. 124,   "I discovered later . . ." Ibid., 369.

pp. 124-125,   "Who am I? . . ." Ibid., 347-48.

p. 126,   "May God in his mercy . . ." Ibid., 370.

p. 128,   "It delighted him . . ." Ibid., 229.

p. 129,   "He never tired of repeating . . ." Zimmerman, *I Knew Dietrich Bonhoeffer*, 228.

p. 129,   "was different . . ." Bosanquet, *Life and Death*, 271.

p. 130,   "Prisoner Bonhoeffer, take your things . . ." Ibid., 277.

p. 130,   "Tell him that for me . . ." Ibid.

Bibliography

Bailey, James Martin and Douglas Gilbert. *The Steps of Bonhoeffer*. Philadelphia: Pilgrim Press, 1969.

Bethge, Eberhard. *Dietrich Bonhoeffer: A Biography*. Minneapolis: Fortress Press, 2000.

Bonhoeffer, Dietrich. *The Cost of Discipleship*. New York: The Macmillan Company, 1961.

———. *Dietrich Bonhoeffer Works, Volume 13*. Edited by Keith Clements. Translated by Isabel Best. New York: Fortress Press, 2007.

———. *Letters and Papers from Prison*. Edited by Eberhard Bethge. New York: Simon & Schuster, 1971.

———. *No Rusty Swords*. Edited by Edwin Robertson. New York: Harper & Row, 1965.

———. *A Testament to Freedom*. Edited by Geffrey B. Kelly and F. Burton Nelson. San Francisco: HarperSanFrancisco, 1990.

———. *True Patriotism*. Edited by Edwin Robertson. London: Collins, 1973.

Bosanquet, Mary. *The Life and Death of Dietrich Bonhoeffer*. London: Hodder and Stoughton, 1968.

Goldhagen, Daniel Jonas. *Hitler's Willing Executioners: Ordinary Germans and the Holocaust*. New York: Vintage, 1997.

Irving, David. *The War Path: Hitler's Germany 1933-1939*. New York: Viking Press, 1978.

Klassen, A. J., ed. *A Bonhoeffer Legacy: Essays in Understanding*. Grand Rapids, MI: William B. Erdmans Publishing Company, 1981.

Metaxas, Eric. *Bonhoeffer: Pastor, Prophet, Martyr, Spy*. Nashville: Thomas Nelson, 2010.

Plant, Stephen. *Bonhoeffer*. New York: Continuum, 2004.

Proktor, Richard. *Nazi Germany: The Origins and Collapse of the Third Reich*. New York: Holt, Rinehart and Winston, 1970.

Raum, Elizabeth. *Dietrich Bonhoeffer: Called by God*. New York: Continuum, 2002.

Robertson, Edwin. *The Shame and the Sacrifice: The Life and Martyrdom of Dietrich Bonhoeffer*. New York: Macmillan Publishing Company, 1988.

Victor, George. *Hitler: The Pathology of Evil*. London: Brassey's, 1998.

Wind, Renate. *Dietrich Bonhoeffer: A Spoke in the Wheel*. Grand Rapids, MI: William B. Erdmans Publishing Company, 1992.

Zimmerman, Wolf-Dieter, ed. *I Knew Dietrich Bonhoeffer*. New York: Harper & Row, 1966.

Web sites

http://www.bonhoeffer.com/

PBS created this site in conjunction with the documentary film about Bonhoeffer that it presented in February 2006, the one hundredth anniversary of Bonhoeffer's birth. Site includes video clips, as well as a short biography, background information, and other study materials.

http://www.christianitytoday.com/ct/2000/117/55.0.html

Christianity Today published this article about Eberhard Bethge a month after he died in 2000. In it he relates how Bonhoeffer regarded his impending execution as somewhat of a relief, since he knew he could no longer be accused of being an accomplice of Hitler.

http://www.pbs.org/bonhoeffer/interview.html

A PBS filmmaker explains why he found Bonhoeffer such a fascinating subject.

http://www.ushmm.org/museum/exhibit/online/bonhoeffer/

A thorough examination of Bonhoeffer's life and work; commissioned by the Holocaust Museum.

Index

Picture Credits